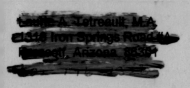

D0426701

From Rejection
to Acceptance

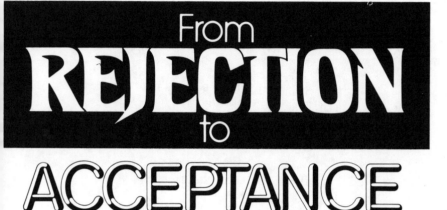

From REJECTION to ACCEPTANCE

Barbara Taylor

BROADMAN PRESS
Nashville, Tennessee

Dewey Decimal Classification: 158
Subject Headings: REJECTION (PSYCHOLOGY) // CHRISTIAN LIFE
Library of Congress Catalog Card Number: 87-6323
Printed in the United States of America

Library of Congress Cataloging-in-Publication Data

Taylor, Barbara, 1931-
  From rejection to acceptance.

  Bibliography: p.
  1. Identification (Religion)   2. Rejection
(Psychology)—Religious aspects—Christianity.
3. Self-acceptance—Religious aspects—Christianity.
I. Title.
BV4509.5.T39   1987   248.4   87-6323
ISBN 0-8054-5045-9

DEDICATION

TO MY PARENTS . . .
  Alice, my precious Mother who, in her childlike way,
    taught me to live, love, and laugh,
  Joshua Bryan, my Father, who taught me to lead,
    forgive, and trust,
TO MY BROTHER . . .
  Bill, who has always been there for me,
TO MY FAMILY . . .
  Jack, Tammy, Tim, Bill, Michelle, Kimber, Timothy
  Bryan, and Blake, who have given me love, accept-
  ance, and support,
TO YOU . . .
  My readers who will make it all worthwhile,
AND TO GOD . . .
  Be glory and praise for His unconditional love and
    acceptance in the Beloved, Jesus Christ, my Lord.

Contents

Rejection . . . A Biblical Perspective

To grasp a biblical perspective on the subject of rejection we must start before time began. This subject is so necessary to spiritual health and well-being that it must be studied from root to fruit, from its beginnings to its full-blown expressions among the human family, and its omnipresence in three worlds—heaven, earth, and hell.

The great, late missionary statesman, F. J. Huegel, left us the legacy of a classic statement: "There is nothing our age so needs as a re-evaluation of evil." That observation was made during the middle years of century twenty! In the face of the diabolical boldness of Satan and his hordes today, what would Huegel say to the church as we prepare for the twenty-first century?

My wife, Barbara, will be sharing with you her personal pilgrimage through the multi-rooted problem of rejection. We are determined to share with you, against the backdrop of severe personal pain, that which we could have learned only one way—through experience. I am providing here a brief background from a biblical perspective, so the reader can have a sense both of direction and position.

A Long, Long Time Ago Before
There Was Time . . .

The first stories familiar to us invariably began with the words, "Once upon a time . . ." Actually this one begins long before that, regardless of how long that "once upon a time" was. To be entirely correct we would have to begin like this: "Once upon a timelessness . . ." When that timelessness gave way to the parenthesis of time no human knows. But the fact is that everyone on this planet has been forced to experience the painful aftermath of what happened in an uncounted eon far from here and long ago.

So will you take the wings of your imagination and fly with me at the speed of thought to worlds shrouded in the midst of unrecorded history? No one was there to take notes except God, and He surely didn't need notes. He was confident to act without a script. He was alone and He was God, quite self-contained, absolutely self-confident, and thoroughly self-complete. He needed nothing or no one else to be what He was and no help to do what He willed to do. He, Himself, was the sole source of all that was, the singular force of that and every eon, and the course along which all that was and was to be followed. The Apostle Paul voiced this truth much later when he wrote in Romans 11:36, "For of Him, through Him, and to Him are all things; to whom be glory forever. AMEN." And there He was, and there They were . . . Father, Son, and Holy Spirit. The foundations of the worlds were about to be laid in the laboratory of timelessness.

In that timeless frame God created the angels, the processes of which remain an unvoiced mystery. We know something, but not much, about these mysterious creatures assigned to do God's bidding. However, that which we do know is vital and reassuring. We know that God has, at least to a measure, entrusted our physical care to these strange, celestial personalities. The psalmist reminds us in Psalm 34:7, "The angel of the Lord encampeth round about them that feareth Him, and delivereth them." Again in Psalm 91:11-12 he says, "For he shall give His angels charge over thee to keep thee in all thy ways. They shall bear thee up in their hands lest thou dash thy foot against a stone."

We also perceive that these creatures have rank and standing in differing measure. Though this is a matter of continuing theological debate I have long since felt quite safe in believing it. We know of two of these angels named in the Scriptures. They are Gabriel and Michael. But evidence is that in ages past there was a third personage in this high class of angelic beings. His name was Lucifer. This was the name given in Isaiah 14:12 to one called the "king of Babylon." Many theologians believe this was none other than Satan himself. Another passage, Ezekiel 28, uses such language as could only refer, many believe, to Lucifer, Satan, or that third angel in the triumvirate. He is also called the anointed cherub that covereth. Be that as it may, what is germane to our subject is what follows in the next discussion.

Rebellion in Paradise

The Isaiah 12 and the Ezekiel 28 passages record this personage of power rising in pomp and pride with intentions to usurp the position that belonged to God. The wilfulness of this great angel is recorded in Isaiah 14:13-14 five times with the words, "I will . . ." That this wilfulness involved pride and vanity is indicated in Ezekiel 28:17: "Thine heart was lifted up because of thy beauty, thou hast corrupted thy wisdom by reason of thy brightness." There was a revolution in heaven occasioned by Satan's diabolical designs for God's very own throne. It was short lived as Isaiah reports, "How thou art fallen from heaven, O Lucifer, son of the morning!" Jesus attests to this in Luke 10:18, "I beheld Satan as lightning fall from heaven." Thus *rejection* touched the heavens and caused myriads of heavenly beings to lose their exalted position in God's realm. *Thus, before time began, rejection as we know it started.* The devil—Satan, Lucifer—served in God's court. He led a revolt against God, violating God's authority. His rejection of God's authority resulted in God's rejection of Satan from heaven's glorious plans. Where was he sent? A vital question! We shall see in the discussion to follow.

The Devil's New Domain

In Isaiah 14:12 Lucifer is said to be "cut down to the *ground.*" In Ezekiel 28:16-17 he is referred to as the covering cherub and is said to be cast, as profane, out of the mountain of God and cast to the *ground.* The word here for *ground* is none other than the word used in Genesis 1:2 for *earth*. So the earth, this physical planet, became the devil's new domain. The Hebrew name for *ground* in both the Isaiah and Ezekiel passages is *erets* which appears first in Genesis 1:2. Right now the devil is in the regions of earth. The rebellion is not over. The address of the battlefront has merely changed. The devil and his angels set up to export rejection and rebellion to every province of the earth.

Rejection and the Human Family

Now we come to recorded history, and that record is rather clear. God created man in His image, after His likeness, and gave to him authority to rule the earth as His extension. Being under authority, man was able to exercise authority. Enter the serpant, i.e.—the devil and rejection are introduced to the human family. The thought of questioning God's word surely had never entered into Eve's mind until the devil mentioned the matter. Rejection moves in circles like these. God's veracity is questioned, then His intentions, and ultimately His very right to rule as God.

The acts of rebellion, induced by the devil, threw off the yoke of Divine authority from the shoulders of man. In gaining a so-called "freedom" promised by the devil, Adam and Eve, representing the whole human family for ages to come, plunged that family into a bondage of rejection and rebellion that has tainted every civilization upon earth. Rejection lies at the root of all human ills.

Beginning with the third chapter of Genesis is a record of perpetual and persistent rejection. With the fall of man there was introduced into the very fabric of creation the universal factor of rejection. Enmity was established in every quadrant, province, and species of the earth. Weeds, thorns, and thistles would express the fact of rejection in agriculture. Agressiveness and violence would reflect rejection among the species of animals. The very essence of sin is rejection. Rejection is etched into the cells of the human mind. The disease of the devil has spread to every person born on the earth until He Who was perfect was born of God in the incarnation—the Lord Jesus Christ. Rejection may be detected in every science man has ever studied, in every culture man has ever founded, and in every realm where man has gone.

In summary I make four observations that will be easily remembered. I feel these are the heart of rejection's history from root to resolution.

First, Rejection Is Rooted in the Person of Satan

With the expression of his malignant intention to change the structure of heaven's government and to usurp the throne of God for himself, his whole being was pervaded with rebellion. In throwing off the yoke of God's authority he accepted the yoke of rejection. In fact, the devil is rejection *personified!* He exudes rejection in attitude, thought process, and speech. He models rejection in every move he makes. To all people who will receive him, he will market rejection. The marks of that insidious marketing are to be found in all the ages of earth and in all the cultures of civilization. It is discoverable in the perpetual tensions among and within the species of every life form, as well as in the fossils and ruins of long dead forms and civilizations. It is detectable in the actions and thought processes of human life from the womb to the tomb. Ultimately, though it may seem to be a cop-out, the recognition of the beginning and the continuing work of the devil in rejection is vital to the resolution of it.

Second, Rejection Is Reflected in a System

It is evident to most that with the rebellion in heaven a number of angels, being deceived by Satan and induced to join him in the rebellion, were cast out with him to the earth. It is also manifest that these creatures form the network of an evil unseen government which would make the worldwide Mafia pale in comparison. Rejection is not only a disease which continues in an unabated epidemic, but it is an intricately-organized system studiously and devotedly perpetuated by unseen persons in the spiritual realm—former angels, now demons. And their instructions and mandates are coming from none other than his infernal majesty, Lucifer, "son of the morning." The reaches of this diabolical system are limitless in this earth. We are born into this atmosphere. Its thoughts are ingrained into the processes of human education from childhood through adulthood.

James described the kind of system of human wisdom that prevails in the earth when he wrote, "This wisdom descendeth not from above, but is earthly, sensual, and devilish [demonic]. For where envying and strife is there is confusion and every evil work" (4:15-16). It is a bitter pill for humanity to swallow, that the only alternative to God's wisdom as revealed in Christ Jesus is wisdom of this world system which, without exception, is earthly, sensual, and demonic.

Satan has franchised rejection and exported it to all continents and islands of the sea. Millions of demons monitor the devil's investments to ascertain that the product (rejection) remains potent and fresh in its poisonous potential. It is produced and distributed with amazing expertise and unopposed persistence. It continues to pollute the very bloodstream of humankind; it opposes love in every expression and intends to replace love with its own prevailing omnipresence. Thus, we are introduced to the system of rejection which networks the world.

Third, Rejection Is Repeated in the Human Family

Though the effects of rejection are observable in every realm we human beings are its primary carriers. It loops again and again in generations, growing more severe with every successive cycle. Whether in its covert or its overt forms, it has affected all of us. It shortcircuits love and confuses communication. It stands like a wall between husbands and wives, children and adults, communities and nations. New chords of rebellion are daily discovered on the organ of rejection. New innovations of destruction grow out of the every-increasing intensity of rejection.

To read the Bible is to engage in a study of rejection from Adam in Eden to John on Patmos. That the human family is the prime carrier is both the bad news and the good news. It is bad news in that we ultimately are to be blamed for its perpetuation but good news in that if the blame lies with us—then the victory lies within the realm of our wills. We as human beings can do something about it! The next paragraph makes this glorious claim.

Fourth, Rejection Is Resolvable Only in Jesus Christ and His Gospel

The disease of rejection was imported from outside this world system. The cure of rejection lies in the glorious truths which surround the coming of God in Christ to this planet earth. He came to establish the antithesis of rejection, love (or acceptance) on the earth. That could only be done in people. The Scripture says in I John 3:8*b*, "For this purpose was the Son of God manifested that He might destroy the works of the devil." Praise be to God He did not specify those works! Thus we can delightedly claim that Jesus came to destroy ALL the works of the devil.

A part of the process of resolving the problem of rejection was in His willingness to become a victim or an object of it. John tells us, "He came unto his own and his own received him not" (John 1:11). Isaiah informs us that He was "despised and rejected of men" (Isa.

53:3). The devil and the world system sought to reject Him who came for mankind's salvation. For the three and one-half years of His ministry from the temptation to the cross we see the death struggle between two systems—rejection and love. Rejection was allowed to take love to the grave. In dying, love lives! Rejection is rejected, defeated, and stripped of its power by the death and resurrection of Jesus Christ. He who was ultimately rejected for us all now ultimately receives the vilest sinner. What a story! "He was wounded for our transgressions, he was bruised for our iniquities; the chastisement of our peace was upon him; and with his stripes we are healed" (Isa. 53:5).

To say that rejection is only resolvable in Jesus Christ is to say it all, but it must be remembered when we speak of Jesus Christ we speak of Him in terms of current history as well as ancient history. The prime fact of history past is that Jesus visited this planet. The prime fact of history future is that He is scheduled to come to planet earth again—such a pivotal matter that it is labeled "our blessed hope" (Titus 2:13). But it must not be forgotten that the most glorious fact of current history is that Jesus is *here* on planet earth in his Body, the Church. It must be remembered that the Church, the Body of Christ, is none other than the *contemporary Christ* made visible to the world. He has no other Body on earth than the Church, the assembly of the redeemed composed of human beings in whom Jesus Christ lives individually. That whole Body of Christ-indwelt beings forms the corporate Body of Christ on earth. What He does must be done in and through His Body!

Almost a quarter of a century ago I discovered the wonder of *Christ in me,* a concept which has affected every part and every moment of my life since that time. And that concept is the precise antidote to rejection, the cure to evil. In a larger way after all these years I am discovering not only the practical implications of knowing Christ in me as an individual, but of knowing the deeper implications of Christ resident, reigning, and released through His Body, the Church. I am discovering that the statement, "Christ in you, the hope of glory," was a reference in the plural. It is Christ in his corporate Body, the Church, that is the hope of glory. This does not diminish the glorious fact that Christ dwells in me as a Person, but rather adds a delightful dimension known as Church life, Body life. "Christ in you" (plural) is the hope!

Thus, to say that rejection is resolvable through Jesus Christ and His Gospel is to say that this must be so in a continuing sense as He presently operates through us individually and corporately. His life is a saving life as powerful as His life was when he walked the hills and valleys of Judea. His physical body was taken into heaven that He, in the Spirit, could inhabit His corporate Body, the Church, and continue to destroy the ongoing works of the devil. Only through His life can this victory be achieved and maintained. Jesus summed it up when he affirmed, "The thief cometh not, but to steal, and kill, and destroy: I am come that ye might have life and have it more abundantly" (John 10:10).

The purpose of Christ is the purpose of the Church. Her grand and prime objective is that through Christ, here and now in the expression which is His Body, the world may know life and life abundantly.

We are to be the receiving station in a world of rejection. We are to be the healing balm in an epidemic of rejection.

Paul exhorted in Romans 15:7, "Wherefore receive ye one another as Christ hath received us, to the glory of God." He had previously stated, "Him that is weak in the faith receive ye, but not to doubtful disputations" (Rom. 14:1).

I want to reiterate these four facts before giving a final word as my part in this volume:

REJECTION IS ROOTED IN THE PERSON OF SATAN.

REJECTION IS REFLECTED IN A SYSTEM.

REJECTION IS REPEATED IN THE HUMAN FAMILY.

REJECTION IS RESOLVABLE ONLY IN JESUS CHRIST AND HIS GOSPEL.

A Final Word

Barbara and I thought that such a biblical perspective as this might be helpful before she related her story. I trust that this will prove a correct assessment.

And now the story with which I have been intimately involved for more than thirty-three years properly entitled *From Rejection to Acceptance.* I have been a part of the problem, unwittingly helping to intensify and complicate the problem, weeping with her in the midst of the problem, and, thank God, at last both a spectator of and a participant in the progressive victory over the problem. It has been a long, hard struggle with hang-ups, strongholds, and reactions of the flesh in me at times hindering the cure. The story you are about to read speaks in concrete, not abstract dimensions. Nothing is spared in speaking of the living or the dead in order to present what is considered necessary information to your benefit.

The purpose of this report is not merely to inspire or inform but toward a resolution of the mystery of rejection that ravages human life in insidious cycles.

I am glad to recommend my wife, Barbara, and her work to you and to be the first to welcome her among the population of a growing group which is being redemptive in our midst, namely, those who have hurt and are willing to become further vulnerable so we might benefit from their hurts reported. But beyond that we rejoice in victory!

JACK R. TAYLOR (better known henceforth as . . . *husband of Barbara!*)

PREFACE
The Root of It All

I want to be out front with you, my reader, at the start. Putting into print what you will be reading has sometimes been very painful to me but at the same time therapeutic. I fondly hope this will not prove to be your garden-variety "self-help book." If it is I have failed. When you are through with this book I want you to feel good about yourself, who you are, and where you are going.

This will not come about by playing "mind games." No matter what the latest conference speaker told you or what the "how-to" booklet said about how simple it was to win the victory, I want to make this most clear: *You will never feel good about yourself until you reach the root of your problems.* The fact is that most of us can find some reason to feel rejection. It is what we do with those first feelings that determine whether life will be overcoming, tolerable, or unbearable.

If we have done the wrong things about our feelings it will be more than evident in later years. As I go about the country speaking to women's groups it is usually obvious to me, as I stand facing a sea of faces, that in many of those lives *something has got to give!* That something may be a flight into fantasy, a retirement into quiet desperation, or a "nervous breakdown"—or maybe even suicide.

I suppose all four of these options crossed my mind, along with some other unspeakable prospects, none of which were viable. So, early on I want to give you some handles in *getting to the root of it all.* At first it may not come easy for you or work in exactly the same manner as it did for me, but I fondly believe my story might help you.

Often the process of rejection begins in a painful and vivid memory stashed away in the deep recesses of our minds. In my case that was so. I recall so vividly something that happened when I was three or four years old, the memory of which was a key in unlocking my mind and which started me on the road of release from my mental and spiritual bondage. I also remember that Jack has recounted that in many cases the healing process begins with recalling a key happening.

The first time I remember that rejection was programmed into the computer of my mind was when, as a three- or four-year-old child, I saw my father strike my mother. My father was a groceryman and had worked for several chain grocery stores before starting his own business. It was about closing time one day, and I can still picture my dad, mother, and Mr. Lowery, the butcher, standing at the front door of the store. As Dad was locking the door, I remember Mother saying something he didn't like, and he slapped her face.

I had no idea how fixed that picture would be in my

mind for years to come, nor did I have an inkling it was the beginning of the "deception of rejection" in my life. Not until recently did I realize that this traumatic moment was the seed that would later produce a bumper crop of rejection in my life. You see, when I saw and heard Dad's disapproval—rejection, if you please—of my mother, I simply transferred that rejection to myself from him. What was programmed into my mind was this thought: *If my father disapproved of my mother, he disapproved of me also.* I identified with my mother and received the rejection she received that day. The lie began, and the deception was planted like a festering seed in my mind. Though a three- or four year-old does not engage in a line of logic, there is, as immature as it may be, a definite chain of reasoning.

My reasoning must have gone something like this: *If my father disapproves of me, there must be a way of winning his approval.* And I, as any child, wanted the approval of my father. How could I do this? By proper performance, of course! And that's how performance-based acceptance (PBA) began in my life.

I cannot tell you how important it has been for me to face that painful memory and trace its destructive path through the years of my life. I found the root of it all! In discovering that root memory I also discovered the little lie that later on became so big as to affect every part of my life.

And so I want to challenge you to begin to pray about finding that key that could begin to unlock the door of the mystery of your bondage. Would you allow me to ask you some questions that I ask women across the country in the hope that you, as many of them, might find that root memory? Is there a particularly painful memory in your past that you deliberately shy away from when it comes before your mind? Are there recurring depressions, spells of bitterness, or waves of resentment that come over you when you began to remember certain occasions in your past life? Are there names of people that, when mentioned, spark feelings that anger, irritate, or depress you? Do you sense that you are holding an "IOU" on someone or some group with the quiet expectation that you will "pay the debt" someday? Do these feelings come out sometimes when you are not expecting them as you are talking to a friend? Do you ever say to yourself or others, "I had forgotten I really felt that way until I talked about it"?

There is much being spoken and written today about the healing and cleansing of the memories, and I would readily admit that there is danger in too much self-questioning. But I must tell from the standpoint of my own experience that, had it not been for my willingness to have my memories probed and being forced to be honest with myself, I certainly would not be writing these words to you.

It may be surprising how early some of those memories began. I remember my husband Jack telling me about a dear, precious preacher with whom he dealt who had recurring and devastating bouts with depression. As Jack challenged him to remember when these feelings that caused such deep depression might have begun and prayed that God would reveal it to him, a strange and remarkable response occurred. A memory sprang suddenly out of the realm of his subconscious mind that was as clear as if it had happened the day before. It was so unpleasant that many years before, he had buried it in his subconscious mind. Jack led him to take the wrappings off that memory, unmask it, face it, and recognize the lies that issued from it. The results were instantaneous and drastic. That preacher had an experience with truth, and the knowledge of the truth set him free. That memory was simply one sentence spoken into the ears of a four-year-old boy. And that sentence, the root lie, had been the source of bondage for more than forty years!

Be patient with yourself. It may not happen to you exactly like this. But give God a chance to uncover any lie programmed into your mind at some time in the past. Stop right here. Spend a few minutes before you read on to pray, ponder, and remember. For some of you the answer is even at this moment knocking at the door, standing beside you, or waiting within you as the key!

BARBARA TAYLOR

1
Love Is the Answer . . .
What Is the Question?

My intention in this book is to be honest. If you knew me you would understand that I would have to strain to be any other way. I have been told I have indications which describe the gift of prophecy, and that prophets have the proneness to be brutally honest. I am no expert on that subject, but I confess that I have the capacity to go to the root of a matter quickly and state the facts as I see them in a plain and sometimes painful manner. That being true, I want to pledge to you, my reader, that I will seek to be as plain, honest, and transparent about myself as I write this book. I honestly feel that this must be the case if I succeed in being the blessing to you that I desire to be.

An honest confession may be bad for the reputation, but it certainly is good for the soul. I hope I will never become a professional either in speaking or writing. The reason for that negative hope is: I believe that my simple reporting of a personal pilgrimage will have more effect than a hundred professional principles. My intentions are to continue to share in plain terms the nature of the background of a victim and the means by which a victim was transformed into a victor by a series of discoveries. This series of discoveries included the *big lie* that we will be discussing in a later chapter, The Deception of Rejection and liberating truths of *love* and *acceptance* to be found in Jesus Christ.

These wonderful truths are not only liberating me from bondage but are enabling me to be used in liberating others from the same bondage. I encourage you to believe that the same cycle can take place in your life—from bondage to liberation to *liberator!*

If you are not a reader of prefaces please break with tradition. Go back and read the preface which is entitled The Root of It All. There you will note that at a given time in my childhood a lie was planted like a seed in my mind. It grew into a fruitful tree—the tree of bondage. All my strivings, anxieties, hostilities, and unfulfilment centered around the lie that I was not loved and had to do something to win and deserve love. You can begin to see how that early on I was programmed to put myself, others, and even God on a performance basis.

As I think back through the years I believe I surely knew that love was the answer. I had read that summary statement of Jesus in Mark 12:30-31 and, in fact, had made it my life passage. I wanted to love God with all my heart, mind, soul, and strength, and my neighbor as myself. I must have tried to do this with every fiber of my being, but I frankly found it impossible. It was then that I made an important discovery—that there were three commands in that passage, not merely two! There were two commands asserted that had to do with

God and others, but *there was one command assumed that had to do with me.* It is easy to overlook because it is at the end of the sentence and is made up of only two words, "as thyself." I was to love as I loved myself! How could I love others, or much less receive or give love to God, when I did not love myself?

I had discovered the origin of my system of lies that had kept me in bondage all those years. I was unloved, unlovable, and chose not to love myself. To further complicate the situation I chose, unconsciously, to spend my life seeking to win approval from God, others, and yes, even myself by performance. All this to no avail!

But how could this suddenly be turned around? How could half a century of wrong thinking be righted? Could I love myself, having rejected myself for all those years, by simply discovering that I didn't? Could hate be transformed into love by a mere discovery? In the midst of these questions let me sound a caution. Though the discovery of the true nature of the problem is absolutely necessary, it must never be mistaken as the solution. So I had discovered that I really didn't love myself. There was tremendous relief in this awareness, but this relief was not in itself the solution. The caution: Never mistake a clarification of the problem for the solution. Go on from there!

The previous questions cannot be answered nor the mysteries solved without a workable definition of love. For me that is best done in Ephesians 1:6*b* which informs me that I am "*accepted* in the beloved." Acceptance is love, and love is acceptance. I cannot love what or whom I cannot accept, and I cannot accept what or whom I cannot love. If I am to love myself, God, and others, then I must find them acceptable. I had already proved that, until I had learned to accept myself, I could not love God or others. NOW AT LONG LAST I HAD DISCOVERED THE BASIS OF SELF AC-CEPTANCE—NAMELY, THE FACT THAT I HAD BEEN ACCEPTED (LOVED) IN HIM. I knew I had *accepted Christ.* That is how we put it. Now, I was seeing, to my shock and surprise, that long before I accepted Him He had accepted me. Now we can see the truth of I John 4:19, "We love him because he first loved us." Too long we have thought only in terms of accept-ing Christ without realizing that acceptance is a two-way street. He had a willingness to accept us infinitely long before we accepted Him. The verse under consider-ation is Ephesians 1:6, but I want you to view the setting of that verse. Read carefully Ephesians 1:3-6:

"Blessed be the God and Father of our Lord Jesus Christ, who has blessed us with every spiritual blessing in the heavenly places in Christ, just as he chose us in Him before the foundation of the world, that we should be holy and blameless before Him, in love; He predes-tinated us to adoption as sons through Jesus Christ to Himself, according to the kind intention of His will, to the praise of the glory of His grace, which he freely bestowed on us in the beloved" (NASB).

Now isn't that mind-boggling? We were in His long-range plans! How can you possibly lose? He chose us in Himself before the foundation of the world that we should be what? That we should be holy and blameless before Him *and* "He predestined us to adoption as sons [and daughters—this gender business has never bothered me!) through Jesus Christ to Himself." The very fact that a person is able to accept Christ indicates He has accepted them beforehand. You and I, if we have accepted Christ, are special people. Even without Him a person is special in His sight as a prospect to receive His love. What does this divine chain lead to and why was it effected? "According to the kind intention of His will . . ." (Eph. 1:5*b*). His will has always been kind, seeking good for every person on the face of the earth, but people bypass His will, and when they do there is always hurt, pain, and remorse. His intentions are always kind. Notice that it was all done "to the praise and glory of His grace" (Eph. 1:6*a*). So what would happen? "Wherein he has made us *accepted in the beloved*" (KJV). The NASB has it "which he has freely bestowed in the beloved." The meaning is the same. "Accepted" and "freely bestowed in the Beloved" are synonymous terms. The NASB capitalized "Beloved." Why? Because Paul is speaking of the family of God. Through Christ we are adopted into the Beloved, the beautiful family of God. We are accepted not only in Christ the Son but also in God the Father.

If we are in Him He has already accepted us. Then we are His workmanship. "For we are His workmanship created in Christ Jesus unto good works which God has before ordained that we should walk in them" (Eph. 2:10). We are his trophies, a proof of His amazing grace, and He never does anything half-way or slipshod. Philippians 1:6 sums it up well: "Being confident of this very thing: that he which hath begun a good work in you will perform it unto the day of Christ Jesus." What he has begun, He is going to complete, finish, and carry to His desired future purpose. Yet, maybe you have never appropriated all He has for you. (This was one of my giant problems. I did not know how to begin to appropriate what He had for me!)

I want to lay before you how I came to begin to accept myself through the Word of God and to look at myself from God's vantage point, not from the old viewpoint of bitterness, defeat, and self-hate. Ephesians 1:6 clearly states that we are ACCEPTED IN THE BELOVED. We are redeemed; we are adopted into God's forever family. We came to Him as Abba, Father, meaning "Daddy" in the Hebrew language. "Abba" was the first word many Hebrew babies learned. "For we have not received the spirit of bondage again to fear; but have received the spirit of adoption, whereby we cry Abba, Father" (Rom. 8:15).

The Mind: The Battlefield

Have you ever heard the statement, "It's all in the mind"? It is generally used to make less serious what is being considered. Well, the fact is; it IS all in the mind. Without the mind there would be no pain as we know it, no anxiety, no loneliness, no rejection. My first step in accepting myself was a step in the mind. I had to consent that the problem was, first of all, in my mind. The word that stood out in my life passage, Mark 12:30-31, was that which referred to loving God with all my

mind. My mind was keeping the rest of me from loving
God, others, and myself.

The Choice: The Beginning of Victory

Within my mind's reach are choices. I must make a
choice and that I did! I chose to take God's Word as
truth over whatever I had previously programmed into
the computer of my mind, over my feelings, suspicions,
intuitions, and thought patterns. What I had chosen to
believe as truth was more real than anything else. Since
I had believed lies about myself, those lies were more
real to me than what God had said in His Word about
me. Now I deliberately choose to take His Word as
THE FINAL WORD about me! The lies may, at times,
float around, looking for a place to land, but as long as
I take His Word as FINAL they remain somewhere in
the atmosphere—totally *incredible!*

In other words, my choice was to TRUST in the
finality of God's Word. For long years I had tried, even
tried to trust, but I found that one cannot try and trust
at the same time. Trying will destroy trusting, or trusting will destroy trying. You cannot try and trust at the
same time. I know. I've tried it.

The choice again is to accept the fact, clearly stated
in the Word of God, that I AM ACCEPTED, i.e.,
LOVED regardless of how I feel, look, think, act or
view myself. I so want you to see this liberating fact that
I want it printed in a line all to itself:

I AM ACCEPTED, I AM LOVED, AND THAT IS
TOTALLY UNCONDITIONAL!

Continued Choices: Necessary for Maintenance

The choice to believe the truth is only a part of the victory, the beginning part! Though an entire chapter will be devoted later to the renewal of the mind, I want to touch on it here. I will again and again refer to the mind as my computer. Like a computer my mind has everything in it that I have seen, felt, thought, perceived, believed, and heard. Believing a lie is like putting the computer on a word search—it only spotlights that which is in accord with the concept sought. In other words, the first lie I believed of my rejection, programmed me selectively to spotlight and remember best what was in accord with that lie.

Therefore, I must preside over the reprogramming of my mind by making deliberate choices in accord with what I have discovered to be the final truth—WHAT GOD HAS SAID! I must work at making right choices when the easier course would be to make the wrong ones because of my feelings, impressions, or suspicions. Sometimes that is plain, hard work!

John 8:32 says, "Ye shall know the truth, and the truth shall make you free." The truth is that God loves me, and I not only have the right but the responsibility to love myself and on that basis to love others. Knowing the truth is like programming data into a computer. I am exposed to the truth, I accept the truth, and I allow it to become a part of my life, thus freeing me to think and act in its light.

So . . . Love Is the Answer!

The reason for the title of this chapter is found in the fact that I knew the answer, but I didn't know the question. Since I didn't know the problem (that I didn't love myself) how could I ask the right question? Right answers demand right questions. I had found the right question! The answer was LOVE, loving myself on the basis that God loved me, loving Him back, and loving others!

And there you have it—the beginning of my journey FROM REJECTION TO ACCEPTANCE. Come along with me!

2

The Deception of Rejection or The Big Lie

Plainly put, rejection is a deception. It is marketed among mankind by our adversary, the devil. In Jack's chapter, "Rejection: a Biblical Perspective," you have seen this. In this brief chapter I will try to outline the false line of logic of the enemy by which people are induced to receive rejection. The line of logic may vary somewhat in differing circumstances, but generally the points will be similar. I will simply list the points and make a brief comment on each one.

"I Am Not Loved"

Now this is tragic news, whether one is one-year old or forty years old. There may be the feeling long before there are words to go with it. The fact is that thousands have the feelings but never give words to the feelings. There is something about this deception that seems to be self-fulfilling. If I believe it I will see that it comes out looking true. Jack says that if we believe a lie from the devil we give him legal right to wrap that lie in a system of deceit that will make that lie for, all practical purposes, look like the truth.

"I Must Be Unworthy of Love"

This second point deepens the pit of rejection. If the people whom I count significant in my life do not act as if they love me I will look for reasons and generally find them, false though they may be. I will say things or accept things said unseriously or in jest that support my suspicions. These are actually some things I said, heard, or thought throughout most of my life: *I am just white trash. I am one big apology. I need to make an excuse for everything I do. I am always wrong. I cannot please anyone. I am dumb. I can't do anything right. I am just no good.* (And the big one . . .) *I will be crazy like my mother one day!*"

You see, when we accept a lie, we also accept other lies which play supporting roles. All other evidences are not admissable in our minds. And the devil continues to cooperate with our minds in conjuring up more and more trash to secure our bondage.

"I Must Perform to Win Love"

This is where thoughts under deceit become actions under deceit, and rejection moves from passive to active. Inner misery becomes active, energetic misery, and others become caught in the storm of rejection. This is precisely how rejection loops in generation after generation. Once thought patterns are translated into activity patterns the forms are set, the trap is secure, and the reactions guaranteed.

Driven by an insatiable desire to please, to be approved, and yet haunted by the continuing fear that I may not be able to accomplish it, makes for a miserable life of trial and disappointment.

One in rejection, while frantically striving for approval, is quietly and desperately confessing, "This is not going to work. Despite all this effort, I will be rejected!" Inevitably this will lead to unconscious actions which will cause reaction in others, and thus the one in rejection can say, "See there, I told you!" Jack would repeatedly tell me that I was like a porcupine or a skunk when in rejection. I guess you would say I acted like a *skunkupine.* When in doubt, I sprayed and when someone tried to help me, they were apt to get stuck with a quill of rejection in the process.

I hope you are aware that what I am saying to you is not on the basis of knowledge from a book on human psychology but from my own personal experience.

"If I Cannot Properly Perform, I Will Be Ultimately Rejected"

This is the dread fear in the back of the mind of one in rejection. As long as there is a faint evidence to the contrary, ultimate rejection is denied. Yet the fear of such drives one to every conceivable means of winning approval.

For many, after years of struggle in the futility of trial and failure, there is the feeling, "What's the use?" and the temptation to give up. At this point, if one does not get counsel, there is the danger of moving into a serious neurosis or near-psychosis of rejection. The problem has become rigid.

Put these points of logic together, and you can begin to understand the depths of misery they spawn. (By the way, I need to state at this point: I do not suggest that everyone has thought out these points as clearly as I have stated them here. What is generally true is that these points have been concluded quietly without protest in the minds of those who experience real or supposed rejection.)

Look at the points again:

"I AM NOT LOVED."

"I MUST BE UNWORTHY OF LOVE."

"I MUST PERFORM TO WIN LOVE."

"IF I CANNOT PROPERLY PERFORM, I WILL BE ULTIMATELY REJECTED."

Now, the crowning blow . . . the coup de grace from the devil . . .

"If I Am Rejected, Then I Must Compensate for This Rejection"

I will be dealing with many of the following qualities under the fruits of rejection. It will suffice simply to list some of them here.

> Hostility
> Depression
> Perfectionism

Defensiveness
Authoritarianism
Accusation
Anger
Self-pity
Bitterness
Jealousy
Workaholism
Alcoholism
Suicidal Tendencies
Promiscuity
Perversion
Self-consciousness
Self-hate
Self-condemnation
Involvement in Occult Practices
Drug Usage
Overeating—Gulttony
Argumentation
Homosexuality

These make up only a brief list of matters into which people move as a result of feelings of rejection. Much behavior otherwise unexplainable may be understood by the attempt to compensate for rejection and the inability to overcome it by normal means. Many of these will be dealt with in the chapter, "A Tree Grows in Barbara" or "The Tree of Bondage."

3

The PBA Dilemma
(Performance-Based
Acceptance)

A definition: Performance-Based Acceptance is approval that is conditioned on one's behavior or merit.

In almost any culture, but especially our Western culture, the matter of behavior is often appealed to by approval or the withholding of it. From the conscious beginning of a child's life that child is appealed to on the basis of performance-approval. We promise rewards for proper behavior and obedience. We say, "Be a good boy and brush your teeth." In reality being a good boy and brushing one's teeth have nothing to do with each other.

The pressure is relentless toward the problem of performance. The child goes to school and is assigned work and given grades. His or her whole system of approval is based on how he or she is graded. Mom or Dad is liable to say, "My, what a good child you are—with all A's!"

Thousands, yes, even millions of people have their parents, mates, children, friends, associates, and even God on what I call here PERFORMANCE-BASED

ACCEPTANCE. It has come naturally with our culture. Very little in our culture encourages unconditional
acceptance. Many will not want to admit they have put
the whole world on such an acceptance basis. They will
not want to admit that this is a deep-rooted problem not
only in their relationships with others but in their relationship with themselves. In such a case it is almost
inevitable that this conditional acceptance is transferred
to one's relationship with God.

It is vital that we understand why we have ourselves,
others, and God on a PERFORMANCE-BASED AC-
CEPTANCE. For the sake of space, and because of the
number of times we will use that term in this chapter
and subsequent chapters, I will refer to it simply as
"PBA." The results of proper understanding will surely
include our willingness to set ourselves, others, and God
free from the conditions we have imposed upon them
and releasing our unconditional love. Thus there will be
healing from the deception of rejection.

Permit me to share my own personal testimony as to
how through prayer my condition was revealed to me,
which was the first step toward a wonderful healing and
liberation. In the midst of this terrifying episode of
rejection that always results from PBA I began to review my life, asking God to help me recall, as objective-
ly as possible, the very essence of my past life. Call that
a kind of Christian self-psychoanalysis if you will.
(Whatever it is called, it worked for me!) As I prayed
I recalled a scene from forty years in the past when I
saw my father slap my mother for the first time. (Remember I referred to this in the Preface.) That memory

had been locked away in my subscious all those years. Though I was not conscious of it, it was there feeding my conscious mind. For you see, when I saw that bit of minor violence against my mother, my little mind perceived the first seeds of rejection. A mind receives impressions without words. For the first time, as I reviewed that painful scene etched on my memory, I also remembered a bit of how I felt. *My father does not approve of my mother. He doesn't like her. Therefore, he does not approve of me or like me either.* My mind had linked me to my mother, and the seeds of rejection began to grow unhindered in my mind. It was then that I unconsciously began the mission impossible of seeking to win my father's approval (which in my mind I did not have) by performance. Thus the many tentacles of PBA began to develop in my life until in my forties the whole world was on PBA (including myself).

I discovered that as a child the whole framework of my theology was shaped by my impressions of and my responses to my father. It is true that our earthly fathers give us our first elementary ideas of what our Heavenly Father is like. One's earthly father is the only understandable association to the mind and emotions of a young child. A preschool child is basically without emotional defenses or understanding. That child has only one way to deal with feelings of rejection, and that is to try to bury them in his subconscious mind. This simply means that, though they may be temporarily forgotten, they will almost completely influence future behavior. As continued feelings of rejection are added to the already buried ones, the influence continues and

deepens. One's whole personality and behavior are ultimately affected. It was certainly so in my case.

Until I was honest enough to admit there was a problem I had no reason to seek help from God or man.
More serious than this was the fact that, until I saw that
the problem was with me, I was convinced that the
whole world around me had the problem. Being a first-
grade teacher by early profession I saw the world's
problem very simplistically as a first grade classroom.
If everyone would do as I said, everything would be fine!
The problem did not stop with me. The rejection problem never does stop with the one feeling rejection. It
continues to recycle in succeeding generations until
someone breaks the deception.

You can see how my "stuffing-and-pretending" process had allowed strongholds to be constructed in my
mind. Place and ground had been given to the devil.
("Neither give place to the devil . . ." Eph. 4:27.) We
will discuss in detail the matter of strongholds in a later
chapter.

The results of this deception of rejection bring about
confused images of God. Strange concepts of God's
supposed assessments and responses to us fill our minds.

I am sure this was the prime reason for my low trust
level. My relationship to and acceptance of the persons
of God the Son and God the Holy Spirit were intact. My
concept of God the Father was blurred, tentative, and
uncertain. I did not know how to trust God as a Father
who would completely care for me. My earthly father
had certainly taken care of my needs as a child, as far
as the material world is concerned, and actually may

have shown signs of love—but with the trauma of what was to happen next, that was all but forgotten. Mom and Dad divorced as I was entering my teenage years. Now the seeds of rejection were growing into fruit-bearing plants, and the divorce watered and fertilized them for greater productivity. This ultimate act of rejection left me wounded and scarred mentally and emotionally, and I am still being healed as I write these words.

Now, back to my low trust level. My father's leaving our home left me with feelings of abandonment and insecurity. Though he continued to care for me as far as my physical needs were concerned, I did not have his presence—the one thing I needed most. His presence was synonymous with his love. In my mind his withholding his presence was the withholding of his love. I could trust him to provide my material needs, but I could not trust him for unconditional love. By the way, my father's determination to care for me physically was based on his relationship to his father. My grandfather was a better student than a provider, a schoolteacher by trade. I remember my father saying, "Dad was a good schoolteacher but a lousy farmer, and you can't eat books!"

My PBA had programmed me to be, among other things, a manipulator. I recall developing the art, during my teen age years, of playing my mother against my father. If I could not persuade my mother to buy the new formal I desired, I would carry the case to a higher court—my father. If neither of them responded properly I would appeal to the highest court, my brother who would always sacrifice for "little sister"!

I have just recalled an episode that is the perfect illustration of my art of manipulation. It happened not long after Jack and I were married. He was in the seminary, and I was working at a major oil company. I have always had this thing about shoes. (Jack recently told me that I had more shoes than Imelda Marcos!) One day during my lunch hour I discovered to my delight this fantastic, unbelievable sample size sale, and would you believe it happened to be exactly my size? I quickly, without consulting anyone, bought seven pairs of shoes!

Now let me backtrack for a moment to report that several days before, Jack and I had discussed a tendency in me with which he was highly impatient. I would start telling him something I had done by saying, "I've done something I shouldn't have done . . .," and then proceed to relate what it was that I shouldn't have done. That conversation had ended by Jack asking me never again to begin a confession in that manner. His suggestion was: if I were going to do something I shouldn't apologize for it but go ahead and do it.

Let me explain that a part of my problem was an intense need to please people (especially my husband), accompanied by the fear that I probably wouldn't be able to. So this wrong use of the apology seemed to be necessary since I would probably wind up being wrong anyway! In fact, my deep feeling was that I needed to make one big apology for even being alive! My father had never disciplined me or directed me about how to behave. So I never knew whether or not my behavior was correct.

Well, back to my story about the shoes. I called Jack to confess what I had done. He answered the phone, and I began the conversation by saying, "I have just done something I shouldn't have done!" There was an ominous "click," and the phone went dead. Jack had actually hung up on me! I thought, *He really didn't do that!* I called again, and he hung up again. (I found out later that he wasn't angry but thought this was the right time to help me break that awful habit.)

I panicked. My manipulative adrenalin flowed rapidly as I called my father to recount the whole story. His immediate reply was, "Baby, don't worry about it. I'll pay for the shoes!" This story tells you at least two things about me. I was still a manipulative little girl, and my father was still accommodating me in that manipulation. I could always count on my dad for the material possessions, but oh how I longed for those blessed intangibles of love, communication, security, and acceptance.

You may be saying as you read this, "Sister, you never had it so good. My father didn't even provide for me in the material area!" You are right in your feelings, but let me make this point. When provision is made in one area and denied in another, the denial seems even more painful than had it been evident in both areas. I am also aware that some of your stories would make mine look minor in comparison. With this painful awareness I am willing to share the depths of my pains with you—with the delightful prospects of the liberation of others like you!

As painful as the episodes I will be recalling were, there are facets which are indeed quite amusing, especially from this side and distance. There are so many considerations about the matter of PBA that are so impossible as to be ridiculous. How much performance is necessary? Who sets the measures, and how will the performance be measured? Will the standards always be changing, or are they set and rigid? How will I know when I have achieved acceptance? What will I have to do tomorrow to achieve it? How long will what I have worked to achieve today last for me? It is possible that the attempt to answer these questions, or the despair resulting from not knowing the answers, will be as destructive as any other part of the process.

My prayer is that God will show you, as He has shown me, why we act with such responses to this insidious PBA and why we feel we must perform like crazy to win approval. The whole matter is really a form of "salvation by works," with the knowledge that as hard as we might try, it will never get us to heaven.

Earlier in this chapter I told you of an episode when my father slapped my mother. More serious to me than the episode itself was the confusion that resulted in me later on when I tried to relate to God as father. How does a father really communicate love and acceptance? Mixed signals from my earthly father caused confusion as I would seek approval from my Heavenly Father.

One of those inconsistencies lay in the fact that, as many times as I had seen my father slapping and choking my mother and even spanking my brother, he never laid a hand on me. This I could not comprehend. He beat mother, spanked Bill, and left me alone with no direction or discipline at all. I am not sure that I understand it yet. The old adage, "Spare the rod and spoil the child," certainly fits me. The contradictory messages I was receiving made me angry. I have told my Dad many times in later years, "If you had spanked me it would have been a whole lot easier to grow up." I have even asked why he had not spanked me. He has no answer to that question, but I do believe that, because of what we both know now, if he had it to do over again, spanking would be order.

I know that one of the ways the Heavenly Father expresses His love is through discipline. Proper discipline gives a child strong feelings of security and acceptance. It is true, whether we understand it or not, that "he who spares his rod hates his son; but he who loves him disciplines him diligently" (Prov. 13:24).

I am learning more about the Heavenly Father's love as I watch my children deal with our grandchildren. Our daughter, Tammy, and son-in-law, Bill, have two children, Kimber and Timothy Bryan. At this writing Kimber is four years old and Timothy Bryan is two. They are both possessors of very determined wills— strong-willed children. (Jack says they are like their maternal grandmother—me!) This is a good quality, even though a bit trying at times, and has pressed Tammy and Bill into becoming strong disciplinarians. They are finding out that the best kind of discipline for one is not necessarily the best for the other. God has made all of us unique and different.

Tammy has found that spanking is not always the best discipline for Kimber. The best method now, on many occasions, seems to be that of sending Kimber to her room with the request that she think about what she has done wrong. She is teaching Kimber to make right choices and to regret and to repent of wrong ones. This method is proving to be more effective, and she has to resort to spanking less often. Kimber told me recently with a great deal of pride, "Tutu (this is my grandchildren's title for me), I haven't had a spanking all week!"

Timothy Bryan is very affectionate and sensitive. He is learning the meaning of the word "No!" The word, spoken with some sternness, usually brings brokenness and tears. He also needs spanking at times and is learning the meaning of being disciplined.

As we watch our children under the influence of God respond to the needs of their children, we are reminded that God in His goodness knows what is best for all of us. After all He created us with needs that only He and our parents can supply.

Our son, Tim, and our daughter-in-law, Michelle, are building into Blake, our youngest grandchild, strong, positive impressions about himself. At this writing he is almost two years old and loves to talk on the phone. Many times Jack or I will ask him, "Who is the most handsome boy in town?" His reply is a loud, "Me!" We feel this is not a seed of pride but simply an optimistic view of himself. Blake is learning that all of the parent figures in his life approve of him and accept him as a person.

All three of our grandchildren are being taught by their parents things that will later help them understand what it is to be God's very own creations. We believe they are not too young to learn that when they do come to know Jesus Christ as their Savior, God, their Heavenly Father will unconditionally accept them, too. We expect such teaching to hasten the day when each of them can make a mature decision regarding their relationships with Christ. Kimber is already talking about Jesus dying on the cross for her sins.

Even before my grandchildren were born I began praying daily that they would never be victimized by the deception of rejection or the tragedy of PBA. I am trusting the Holy Spirit to show them who they really are as valuable human beings now cared for by the unconditional love of God and who they will become as God's very own special creations in Christ. As they trust their parents and see God imaged in them, they will learn that He, too, is trustworthy and that what He tells them in His Word can be trusted.

Excuse the musings of a grandmother about her grandchildren and thanks for indulging me! I suppose I am close to being obsessive about providing them an environment in which they will know, on a continuous basis, the meaning of unconditional love and acceptance.

The PBA is with all—yes, PBA has struck in almost every life. Parents will either be the means of continuing the tragedy or perpetuating blessed answers and solutions. If parents are loving, caring, and trustworthy, a proper picture of God will dissolve feelings of rejection. Parents are apt to be more loving if feelings of rejection can be dealt with in them. You who are parents, "It is not too late to break the loop of rejection in your family tree!"

Have I talked enough about PBA for you to detect whether or not it is a part of your problem? Do you find much of your time spent being concerned about how others feel about you? Do you ever find yourself feeling despair that you have not pleased yourself or someone else? Do you have periods of extreme depression over poor performance? Do you become so disappointed in others that you tend to reject them? Are there times when you have total unrest in relating to yourself? The answers to these questions may form some clues as to the real nature of your problem.

One of the profound problems in this whole affair is that most of us tend to deny we have a problem. This very denial denies us needed help, and the real problem becomes more severe. You need to know that it is all right to have problems. All human beings have them! The important matter now is to ask, "What am I going to do about PBA in my life?" As you answer this question you will discover that God will bless in both directions—those who have you you on PBA and those you have on PBA. May I make some suggestions for homework between this chapter and the next?

First, admit that you have a problem and honestly face the influence that your PBA is having on your relationship to yourself, others around you, and especially God Himself.

Second, if you have been blaming others, take responsibility for all your actions, deliberately taking everyone off PBA (starting with yourself).

Third, accept God's unconditional acceptance of yourself as a child of His and allow Him to take away guilt that has extended your problem.

Fourth, begin to review portions of God's Word that describe the true identity of all saints and claim them for yourself.

Fifth, begin to allow God's Word to reprogram your faulty thinking. (Eph. 1:3-6, 2:10; 2 Cor. 5:17; Rom. 5:1).

Sixth, allow God to begin the liberating processes in your life.

Remember this one Scripture as you meditate on God's attitude toward and assessment of you: "Being confident of this very thing, that he which hath begun a good work in you shall perform it unto the day of Christ Jesus" (Phil. 1:6). With this in mind be assured that you can rely on the fact that you are loved and accepted by your Heavenly Father. This is the place to begin for total victory over rejection.

4

The Rejection Syndrome

Rejection may be defined as a feeling or action conveying unfitness, disapproval, or unworthiness. A *syndrome* suggests a condition that has become rigid, fixed, or chronic. We have discussed rejection as a common problem which varies in seriousness in different people. I want to deal with the rejection syndrome in this chapter.

Rejection is an almost universal game thousands of families play. It proves to be much like the game, "Pass It On." Rejection recycles from generation to generation from parents to children. As it continues to be passed on, it tends to become more and more serious with each passing generation. As rejection repeats itself another deadly game is played which might be called "reverse the blame" as children blame their parents but repeat with their own children what they blame on their parents.

The rejection syndrome has its roots in the Garden of Eden, as Jack indicates in his chapter "Rejection: A Biblical Perspective." These poisonous games were first noted in the Garden of Eden. Satan had been rejected by God in heaven, and he passed it on in the realms of the earth. He marketed it to Eve as he planted suspicions in her mind about the intentions of God for her life. Her act of disobedience was based on a suspicion the devil had given her that God had withheld something from her.

Eve rejected God's authority and passed it on to Adam. When God arrived on the scene after they had sinned, the game of "reverse the blame" began. When Adam was confronted he simply alibied, "The woman whom you gave to be with me, she gave me of the tree, and I ate" (Gen. 3:12). (In reality Adam was not only reversing the blame to Eve but to God Himself!) As Eve was faced with the sin, she responded with these words, "The serpent deceived me and I ate." From that time to the present every person born on this planet has experienced rejection in some form or another.

Rejection is an epidemic among mankind. If we will be honest with ourselves and each other we can stop these devil-created games before we pass them on to our innocent children. We can break the chains of rejection that has had our families bound in slavery to a hellish master. We can be set free to worship and serve the Lord as we were made to do. We can then know the truth of our genuine identity and acceptance in the Beloved.

Honesty had to be the choice for me. It hasn't been easy or without pain. I have found that being honest with myself and facing the truth are about the hardest things I have had to do. The truth hurts because it reveals the wretchedness of self. In fact I had to reach the point of desperation in my life before I could face the truth about my rejection syndrome.

We have discussed in the previous chapter the problem of performance-based acceptance and how it affects all our relationships, especially those relating to our parents and God. The same revelation that caused me to realize where and when PBA began in my life also opened to me the fact of my deep-rooted rejection. In Chapter 3 we discussed the fact that performance-based acceptance and rejection are bound together by the enemy and are somewhat synonomous.

Dr. Charles Solomon in his book, *The Rejection Syndrome,* writes that rejection is a force destructive to the personality. I can say "Amen!" to this because my whole personality was affected by the negative and critical strongholds of rejection. I remember how negative and critical the atmosphere was in our home. My personality was so negative that I always saw a signal light as a red light. Not until I was delivered from a stronghold of negativism did I begin to see green lights. I had a critical spirit and even hated critical people because I hated my own critical personality.

Dr. Solomon also observes that rejection often takes the form of hatred for someone else. I can relate to that. There were times when I felt plain hate for my parents. Friends and associates were not excluded from these feelings of hate, either. A strange fact about the rejection syndrome is that no one around is immune from its hostility. It would appear that our intimates who love us the most might be safe, but often the exact opposite is true. Those we love the most, those who are most committed to our welfare, seem to be the first upon whom we vent our rejection hostilities.

While overt hatred was a part of my rejection syndrome, Dr. Solomon states that such is not always the case. A covert form of rejection fully as devastating is what he calls "smother love." This leads him to define rejection as the absence of meaningful love at best and the wanton disregard of another person and his needs at worst. I can relate to the latter but not to the former.

My dad's act of leaving us meant to me the absence of love. With his leaving, love had left. The long-term results of this were carried over into my marriage. I unconsciously transferred my feelings of rejection at their worst from my father to my husband. Every time Jack would leave for a meeting I would allow myself to believe he was leaving me. Consequently, the trips to and from the airport were almost unbearable. When he left I would seek to "get back at him" in advance for leaving me. When he returned I would dump everything on him for having left me.

Rejection occurs when acceptance is contingent upon a satisfactory performance. I can relate to this because one of the results of my rejection was a compensation with perfectionism. Since I seemed to have no one who cared enough to actively approve of me I tried to act and think perfectly.

Here I am discussing the rejection syndrome from a autobiographical standpoint. That is my point of reference—how it has been with me. I know that when love is withdrawn knowingly or unknowingly the syndrome begins to take shape. And once the syndrome is in shape we tend to make rejection the universal response. It is more or less of a "catch-22" situation. We act in such a manner as to guarantee rejection from those around us, and then we wallow in it. I experienced rejection with my parents, husband, children, friends, church members, and others.

Sometimes a person in rejection feels that pressures around him/her are denying him/her the right to become a person. This was my feeling in Jack's pastorates for the first twenty years. I simply felt I was not allowed to be me. Of course, people were not standing around blocking my path to being who I was, but that is how I perceived it. The results were the same as if folks had formed committees designed to keep me from being me! I have an idea that many people whose spouses are in recognized positions have a problem like this. I sometimes received rejection when introduced as "the pastor's wife," or "the evangelist's wife," or "the author's wife." I asked a friend one day why I couldn't be introduced simply as her friend. Isn't that a miserable way to look at something that ought to make you feel grateful? Yes, but that is how it was.

We have already talked about placing blame as one of the diabolical games people in rejection play. I was busy blaming my parents who were still playing the games of rejection. An irony about this was that they were not even aware of the war being waged about them, or the enemy, or the games they were playing. They had never even heard of the deception of rejection or of performance-based acceptance. They, themselves, were filled with guilt, fear, suspicion, resentment, bitter-

ness, and self-pity, as well as other strongholds stem-
ming from rejection. Had you asked them if they were
rejecting their children they would have looked at you
in stunned surprise and probably wondered what you
were talking about. They were busy merely trying to
survive. And, in those days, had you asked me if I were
in rejection, I would probably have moved into hostility
and replied, "Absolutely not—but the whole world is
rejecting me!"

This is why I believe God is allowing me to share my
story. There are thousands of families who need to
know the truth. My prayer is: May the Holy Spirit show
you who read this book how you can relate and identify
with us and come to the end of our story with a new
beginning for yours.

I want to share with you one of the most exciting
sidelights about the rejection syndrome. Once it begins
to heal and light begins to break through about the
nature of it, there comes about an understanding of the
needs and reactions of others that those who are not in
rejection never understand. I write this is praise to God,
but because of my past in rejection I seem to have the
ability to spot rejection a mile away. Jack remarks that
there are times when I discern something about someone when he is as "dumb as a duck." Since I have begun
to be liberated I have found that just as bondage loops
in generations and environment, so does liberation. *Liberation is catching!* Let's start an epidemic. Let's you
and I be carriers!

When I began to discern the real nature of my problem and the futility of blaming others, my first steps

toward healing took place. If the problem were originating with someone else, that put healing out of reach for me. Bad news! But as I owned the blame for my own situation, regardless of how, where, and when it originated, that brought the solution close, as close as my very own mind and will! You will see the story unfold of how God turned my rejection around and began to cause liberation to flow. My mother, before her homegoing, became a beautiful and free person, a joy to all who were around her—nothing short of a miracle.

And my father—that is quite a story! Daddy was one of nine children. He stayed on the farm while his brothers and sisters went off to work and college. His relationship with his father, my grandfather, was not good. Daddy was beset with dreadful feelings of insecurity and inferiority resulting in much rejection. His response to these feelings of rejection in later life was toward alcohol. There were brief periods of sobriety interspersed between devastating episodes of drunkenness, fighting, and near tragedies of varying kinds. In one of these, my second stepmother shot my father five times and was preparing to load the gun for another round when he begged her to call the doctor instead. I have seen my stepmother move every stick of furniture out of the house to spite my father. I have come home to find blood on the floors, ceiling, and walls with daddy and his wife injured at each others' hands. This was a finished product of the rejection syndrome. You can imagine what this programmed into me.

Of course, this rejection had begun to peak many years before Dad and Mother divorced. I was twelve years of age, impressionable and sensitive. I then began to feel then a mixture of blame and anger, guilt and self-condemnation. I felt, *They have surely done this (divorce) because of me.* I felt unloved and unwanted. My parents were not saying, "We're rejecting you, Barbara. We're against you. We're sorry that you were born to us." They didn't have to say that because their actions, as far as I was concerned, were speaking more loudly than words ever could have. Rejection seemed to loom large in all they didn't say and all they didn't do.

Back to my mother. (Jack says I write like I talk, moving from one subject to another, but has finally given up and has consented to let this book be me!) Mother also had deep-down feelings of rejection. She was a twin, and her twin was born dead. Somehow from the time she could begin to put ideas together, she began to blame herself for the death of her twin. If I have heard her say it once, I have heard her say fifty times, "I should have died. I shouldn't have lived. I didn't have the right to live and my sister die." That was her litany of self-imposed guilt. She never seemed to stop long enough to think that God had a reason for sparing her, for allowing her to live, for keeping her in the world. I am glad to say that before she died a few years ago she began to experience acceptance and love, and the last days of her life were characterized by a totally new perspective on life. She was joyful and a joy to all around her.

You see, my mother's mom died when mother was two months old. Her father died when she was eleven years old. Isn't it strange that mother and I began to experience serious rejection at about the same age? At any rate, mother began to build her own private torture chamber over the death of her twin and the deaths of her mother and father. These circumstances, already fertile ground for the seeds of the rejection syndrome, were complicated by the fact that mother was to spend the next years with a brother and sisters among whom she felt no acceptance, was given no responsibility, and achieved no sense of identity. She felt herself to be a total misfit. Her rejection was more covert than overt, but nevertheless real and deep. When she and Daddy married, they came together carrying the tangled threads of rejection. It was a marriage of sorts for seventeen years. They fought and screamed, slapped and cussed, and drank and pouted in an ever-worsening downward spiral until their marriage hit the rocks in the divorce court. The rejection syndrome had looped and would live to loop again!

But, praise the Lord, we have seen that tragic looping cease and a dramatic healing in all begin! My mother was a Christian and though I was saddened at her sudden death, I know where she is. Before she died she gave me permission to use any or all of her story in the book she knew I would be writing. My father is now a Christian, a praying man, active in church, and has consented to my using these painful memories of the past to help liberate people.

To show you the magnitude of the miracles of healing in my parents I want to go even more deeply into the problems. It will help you to see the nature of the rejection syndrome. My mother was increasingly mentally unstable. This was complicated by the fact that she had to work to eat, was all alone, and becoming more and more physically disabled. She had lost all the money she had received in the marriage settlement in a losing business proposition. She lived from hand to mouth. Though she was trained as a PBX operator, she soon reached the point where she could no longer stand the pressures of a full-time job. She simply could no longer cope physically or mentally. Her mental condition worsened. She began to hallucinate, became paranoid, and barricaded herself into a room against imagined attackers. Those phantom enemies were plotting her death, even trying to poison her, she thought. My brother called me, and Jack and I went to Fort Worth to rescue mother. That was surely one of the saddest and most difficult days of my life. I had to take responsibility for having my mother committed to a state mental institution. This was to happen five times. She could not function with reason among people. Within the controlled environment of the mental institution mother would get better and be released. Back out into the real world she would experience rejection again, some of it real, most of it imagined, but with the same results. It was back to the mental institution four more times.

During that time I realized that my brother and I had always seemed to reverse the roles with our parents. We were not only forced to be responsible for ourselves but for our parents as well. That is the reason why I often felt (though I may never have verbalized it) that I would have been better off without parents.

Then I also began to realize I had been an extension

of my mother's problem (as well as my father's) instead of a part of the solution. Yes, in my own mind I had reasons to feel resentment for having to carry my own load. That resentment seemed to be more reasonable since I had the weight of my mother's care on my back. But the cold, hard fact was that mother was not feeling any acceptance from her daughter! At that point I made a very important decision to accept my mother as she was and love her unconditionally. In the next chapter I will talk about the methods God led me to adopt with my mother and my father, which God used to begin their liberation.

In my rambling description you have surely seen a textbook case of the rejection syndrome in its beginning stages, in its full-blown influence, and thankfully in its healing processes.

Stay with me. The story gets better, and you'll love the ending!

5
Freedom Through Forgiveness

I may have left you in mid-air about my relationships with my father and mother, but it was because I wanted to deal with the turning point in those relationships. That turning point occurred when I said to myself, *Barbara, you must accept and forgive your mother and father, no matter what they have done.* At that point I faced the fact that, if I were ever going to get better in relating to myself and others, I had to forgive those I held responsible for rejecting me.

As I reflect on that turning point I can now see clearly at least four reasons why forgiveness was a must.

First, if I were ever going to be completely right with God, I had to practice forgiveness. That is made completely clear in Matthew 6:14-15, "For if you forgive men their trespasses, your heavenly Father will also forgive you. But if you do not forgive men their trespasses, neither will your Father forgive your trespasses." Could that be any plainer? Of course, the good news is that God will readily forgive us, even of long-term unforgiveness on our part. "If we confess our sins, he is faithful and just to forgive us our sins, and to cleanse us from all unrighteousness" (1 John 1:9).

Second, as I wrote previously, my own healing waited on my willingness to forgive. There is a redeeming feature to the discovery that the problem rests with *me.* If the problem is with me, then the solution can begin with me! I used the word "healing" in the first sentence of this paragraph because my conviction is that all forms of healing can and do occur in forgiveness. I believe it will be proved that certain forms of serious physical maladies begin, worsen, and feed upon damaging emotions which issue from unforgiveness. It is true that like hate, unforgiveness is an acid which does more damage to the vessel in which it is stored than the victim on which it is poured. I had to face the fact that my emotional and spiritual, as well as physical, healing waited on my determination to forgive. I will deal with the physical effects of unforgiveness later on.

Third, the healing of those victimized by my unforgiveness waited on my choice to forgive. It is as if, when we have unforgiveness, we build two prison cells: one for ourselves and one for the persons we refuse to forgive. When we declare forgiveness, the key fits both prison cells, and the prisoners are ready for release. If you don't believe this works, I can only tell you what it did for me and challenge you to try it in your circumstances.

Fourth, the healing of others not related to my circumstances waited on my forgiveness. Had I not begun to move toward victory, the many people I have seen begin their journey to freedom might never have been helped.

I can assure you there are people all around you, and many you have never met in other places, who will reap a part of the harvest of your healing. God is ready to draft all the liberators He can find to command the pharaohs presiding over thousands of believers in bondage, "Let my people go!"

Now, back to my parents and living proof of what can happen when forgiveness is injected into a sad and sick situation. I will deal with my mother first. You will remember from the previous chapter about mother's eventual diagnosis of serious mental illness. I was told she was a "paranoid schizophrenic." I had only heard about it before but do not remember having met anyone with that kind of illness. I now believe it is a sort of catch-all diagnosis with vague borders and unsure cures. Nevertheless I was urged to believe mother was that way, that there was no cure, and that I might as well make up my mind to live with it the rest of her life. So medical science had given me its decision and had announced its total helplessness.

One more door shut in our faces! Praise the Lord for shut doors! If we found the answers to our dilemmas anywhere else we would never see the miracle of His power in operation. Isn't it interesting that God generally does not perform a miracle until the situation is beyond all human hope? Jesus chose to perform a miracle only when "Lazarus was dead." In my case with mother "Lazarus was dead."

With the unavoidable conviction that I must forgive my mother, coupled with the realization that with all I was willing to do for mother, I was more ashamed of her than anything else. Repenting of both unforgivenss and the sin of shame, I was wonderfully forgiven. I found out quickly that when we work in line with God's desires, with our hearts right with Him, He (God) goes to work.

I wanted to get mother out of the mental hospital, but I had two problems. First, I was not financially able to care for her in the manner her condition demanded. And, second, it would not have been wise to have her in our home at the time. I informed mother's case worker of my desires to take her out of the hospital and put her into a nursing home. Mother was not yet sixty-five and thus could not receive Social Security benefits. But God began to work! Through a timely change in the Social Security rulings mother was able to receive full benefits before the minimum required age, move into a lovely nursing home, and have it all paid for by her Social Security benefits. Praise the Lord, He not only answers prayer, He answers forgiveness!

Despite the fact I had forgiven mother I finally admitted to myself that I really didn't love the responsibility of caring for her that had been thrust upon my shoulders. I still wanted a distance between me and her. "Haven't I done enough, Lord?" I asked Him repeatedly. "Haven't I gone the second, third, and fourth miles?" Was I going to have to forgive her literally "seventy times seven"? But the Holy Spirit was relentless in His work of implementing forgiveness. I was going to visit mother about every two or three weeks. That was not enough! She was better but not much better. She was still an emotional recluse, sitting alone in her room and reading or just staring and thinking. She never left her room except for the library or meals. Neither did she enjoy the craft periods she was required to attend. I had to face the fact that she would probably not improve without my commitment to give her more of my time.

My head is hard, and my will is strong. If you don't believe it, ask the Lord and Jack! Well, the Lord and I fought over this situation for a long time. My schedule was already full with busyness a pastor's wife does. And besides this I had recently become active in a Bible study fellowship, felt I needed it, and was enjoying it immensely. In addition to this I felt I was growing spiritually as a result of the Bible study fellowship. But if I were to obey God something would have to give! Obedience is better than sacrifice, but most of the time obedience requires sacrifice. God and I fought this battle for about six weeks and, as I suspected, God was able to "outlast" me and win the battle. Hallelujah for battles He wins and we lose! My next step of obedience would mean that I would give up the Bible study fellowship and spend that morning of the week with my mother! You see, when revival came to Jack's life, the Lord directed him to Ephesians 5:18, "Be ye filled with the Spirit." When revival came to my life, God pointed me to Ephesians 6:2, "Honor your father and mother, which is the first commandment with promise." God carried me straight to the root of my disobedience and unforgiveness.

So Wednesday became "Mother's Day" . . . the weeks I was not on the road with Jack. I would check mother out of the nursing home and do with her exactly what she wanted to do. We would have a hamburger and a milkshake and then go to the park and ride the train together, like the little children we never had the privilege of being.

And through these hours of our days together mother began to see, miracle of miracles, that somehow I really did love her! Perhaps for the first time in her life she came to realize that someone, and her own daughter at that, was beginning to receive and forgive her unconditionally. Surely through this realization she recognized that God also loved her and had loved her all along. At that time I did not comprehend all the chemistry that was going on in her, in me, and most of all between us. I was merely following what I believed God wanted me to do. I no longer thought about the "oughtness" of it or that it was something I had to do because no one else would do it. It was becoming a ritual and a routine but a pleasant one at that! In a sense it was becoming an experience of worshiping the Lord.

You may be thinking, *Good grief, she's making a big deal out of that. I've done all kinds of things for my mother and father and loved ones.* But you must remember that these were really the first experiences my mother and I had known of this kind. She . . . and I were coming from rejection. We had both experienced this rejection at the hands of our own flesh and blood and had retaliated with a rejection of our own. Mother and I were *externalizing* acceptance and forgiveness while God was *internalizing* them.

From our repaired relationship and hours of meaningful fellowship my mother began to glow and grow. The last ten years of her life she lived in the city where she had grown up. She had wanted very much to live there and had looked forward to the move with keen excitement. The Lord led us to just the right nursing home, and there she blossomed in every way. To a life terribly short in the simple joys of life those joys began to come. Mother began to have fun and developed a wonderful sense of humor. She enjoyed her friends in the nursing home and was the "official" server of the "morning coffee." She enjoyed her grandchildren, and they enjoyed her.

I once asked her how she got rid of demons that once harassed her. She simply replied that she had told them to leave and then asked Jesus to take all those evil things away. She said that she realized if Jesus didn't do something she would have to spend the rest of her life in that awful condition. I continued to give mother my time, as did my family. We would have her in our home for special days and she proved to be an increasing delight.

Mother had moved from an incurably ill paranoid schizophrenic to a delightfully happy, healthy, and loving bearer of God's Good News! She had developed under the Spirit's nurture into a beautiful person. In her last few years she had encouraged and helped so many of the nursing home patients that I had to conduct a ministry of consolation at the home after her passing. You would have thought, by listening to the testimonies of the residents, that she was Mother Teresa.

She almost made it to her seventy-seventh birthday, which would have appropriately been on Mother's Day that year. But a few days before that, as Jack and I had settled down for a few days in the mountains of Colorado, our son, Tim, called to share with us that mother had quietly gone to heaven in her sleep the night before. Of course, I was saddened at her going but had fleeting thoughts of how tragic it would have been if she had gone before we had known those days of love, forgiveness, and healing. And, as if God wanted to make one last crowning "Amen!" to our relationship, he made her face as beautiful to look upon in death as it had been in the last years of her life. In the casket that day, as we viewed her form for the last time, her face all but shown with miracle light. She looked so natural that I felt liberty to allow our little granddaughter to see her, and her response was that she wanted to touch her grandmother. How thorough and beyond all our expectations are the processes of God!

Now to my Father. In my mind I surely had more to forgive him for than my mother. After all, he was the one who had slapped her that day, that act which had been the primary seed of the dread rejection syndrome in my life. He had been the one who had left her—and me. But all my rejection, hatred, and shame of him had done nothing toward delivering him from his terrible drinking habit or a life of regret and devastation. What I faced with Mother, I faced with Daddy: that he would surely be no closer to healing until I released him from the bondage of unforgiveness in which I had him chained. After determining to forgive him and declaring it so, I did a simple thing. I wrote him a letter. First of all, the very act of writing was a sacrifice. I have little trouble talking, but writing is a different matter. That is one reason why I have waited so long to set down on paper what I am writing to you. In that letter to Daddy I asked him to forgive me of all the resentment and hatred I had felt for him, of which he wasn't even aware.

I sent the letter to him for Father's Day instead of a greeting card. I began to call him, and we began to share our lives with him as a family. Up to this point the only times we would communicate would be when he was drunk and wanted to talk. Otherwise—almost total silence! I began telling him that I had prayed for him for many years. I shared with him the pent-up hostilities I had felt for him and asked him to forgive me. Of course, he accepted my apologies and forgave me without hesitation. (The fact is that most of it was a total surprise to him. He was totally unaware of the rejection that had issued from him, as most folks are!)

I now insert in this part of my story a word that will show you how serious I was about Dad's getting right. When Jack was in Southwestern Baptist Theological Seminary in Fort Worth, where Daddy lived, we were expecting our first child. During the time of my pregnancy I would often pray, "Lord, if it takes my life or that of my baby to straighten out my daddy's life, do whatever it takes." You have to admit, that this was an urgent, almost panicky prayer. I can tell you, dear reader, I did not realize how grave my prayer was! Our baby was born and in three days God called him back home. In the back of my grieved heart I knew that God had answered my prayer but I thought, *How long will it be before I see the results in my daddy's broken life?* I have never blamed God for calling back our baby; neither did I resent my father for perhaps being the occasion of it. I did, however, carry a heavy burden of guilt about my prayer. When Dad came to the hospital, I did confess to him what I had prayed. After he had gotten right with God, I asked him if he thought that this prayer had any influence on straightening out his life. He assured me that it did, that it had a profound effect on him.

Let me backtrack again before I move on to another prayer I prayed for my daddy. At one time Daddy owned a tavern (a beer joint) and a liquor store. Both businesses were located in the same building with a wall between them. I prayed repeatedly, "Lord, please put that joint out of business whatever it takes, even if it's a tornado, but please spare Daddy!" Would you believe that along came a tornado and blew that tavern all to smithereens, a real "act of God"? God had specifically answered my prayer and had destroyed the beer joint but had left the liquor store totally intact with almost nothing broken. I should have been more specific and included the liquor store! (The next weeks were spent by Daddy and his third wife in the liquor store literally drinking the shelves dry!)

So the Lord's answers to my prayers regarding my daddy continued on schedule. Rather suddenly we all noticed that something seemingly happened to Daddy. He was sober and it lasted. He was changed! He began to attend church and became interested in other people and their salvation.

He now attends church regularly and has an hour on his church's prayer ministry which he rarely misses.

Our fellowship grows sweeter and sweeter. He recently shared with us about the night he made his "big turn." It had happened about fifteen years before. He had been on a big drunk. (Dad never thought of himself as an "alcoholic"—just a plain, miserable drunk!) He had driven his car in his drunken condition all the way across town without being conscious of it. He came to by the side of the road where he had parked, and there was a policeman by the side of his car. It so happened that the policeman knew him and escorted him home. After that series of miracles Daddy determined to pray, "God, if you will help me, I will never take another drink as long as I live!" He was instantaneously cured, healed, and sobered and has been so ever since. He was delivered from the stronghold of alcohol.

He has lived through heart problems, he now wears a pacemaker, and continues to live joyfully for the Lord and with concern for others.

Just as God did with Mother, He crowned the story with something for "good measure." Recently, my aunt, Daddy's only remaining sister, died. She had requested cremation and her family had granted the request. Several weeks later her ashes were returned to the family burial plot. I was across the country working on this book and was deeply involved in the doing of it. I had not planned to make that interment, and no one had expected me to attend. But in the midst of my work I began to sense a desire and an inner demand to make that meeting. I could not understand that inner compulsion, but I stopped my writing and study, caught a plane, went to my father, and then drove fourteen hours to and from that service. I had no idea why that inner compulsion had moved me until in that service at the graveside, my dad testified to the group there, "I have something to say. The next time you come here will be for my burial, but don't be sad, because I am right with God. I am really right with God. I am ready to meet my Maker." You cannot possibly realize the significance of that moment for me and all those there. Nephews were there that Dad had drunk and womanized with. His testimony will surely bear fruit with them. Before we left the graveside several of my cousins asked me to pray for them!

And the story goes on. You can see why I have called this chapter "Freedom through Forgiveness." The circle of forgiveness is ever-widening and ongoing. You can imagine how these miracles are enhancing my own freedom. The strongholds continue to fall and tumble in like the walls of Jericho. It will be ever so! When we begin to forgive, others begin to become free, and when they begin to get free, we get more and more liberated.

6
Rejection and Strongholds: Defining and Detecting

Up to now I have approached rejection almost totally from the point of reference of my testimony. I have sought to be honest in allowing you to see rejection in its inception, continuation, and devastation in my own personal life. If there is one facet of my ministry that seems to draw more discussion than any other it is that I am willing to be honest. While that point of reference will continue you will notice that with this chapter I will try to do more teaching, more how-to, and more practical procedures.

Now, I want to discuss rejection in another light, as a spiritual stronghold. But before I do, here's more of my testimony.

In earlier days of my spiritual pilgrimage I had basic knowledge of a few realities. First, I knew I was saved and that heaven was my destination. I had a ticket to heaven but no passport to joy. Second, I knew that, according to Colossians 1:27b, Jesus Christ, by the Spirit of God, was alive inside me. (The verse simply affirms "Christ in you, the hope of glory.") Third, I knew that my right and responsibility as a Christian was to be filled with the Holy Spirit (Eph. 5:18). Years ago when Miss Bertha Smith touched my life with her wonderful ministry, I discovered the Spirit-filled life. One of the strong points of her ministry in this area had to do with getting our sins "confessed up to date." This involved making a sin list. I understood this quite well since I considered myself "the chief of sinners." My list was long and heavy. I was all too glad to cooperate in getting rid of all my sins. What was next?

Miss Bertha was staying in our home for one particular conference, and I remember asking her, "How can I stay filled with the Spirit?" Her answer was simply that I was to appropriate. I was a first-grade teacher, and the word "appropriate" was not a first-grade word, so I didn't get it. During that conference I fully confessed my sins "up to date" and did all that Miss Bertha suggested I had to do to be filled. While there was temporary joy there soon was a realization that many of the same thought processes and "old deeds of the flesh" were still all too much with me.

I was like the preacher who was praying in the presence of his wife, "Oh, Lord, please fill me with your Spirit." She was heard quietly praying in the background, "Watch him, Lord, he leaks!" I leaked continuously and seriously. The fact is, at times I poured! My frustration and confusion mounted so I could not seem to appropriate the blessed implications of this blessed Spirit-filled life. Then I began to recognize that those areas of repeated sin were entrenchments of the enemy in my life, strongholds, if you please. Those were areas of spiritual warfare, and the devil was influencing the war from behind the lines. The word "stronghold" is a New Testament word which means "hard place," "entrenchment," or "fortress." It is an area of potential negative influence where Satan and his demons have some freedom to spread their lies and extend their devilish plans. *Webster's Dictionary* states that a stronghold is a "fortified strong place." It may involve entrenched habits, life patterns performed habitually, or thought processes out of accord with both reason and the Scriptures. After Jack began to teach about strongholds it became clear to me that this was the only explanation for these areas of repeated defeat in my life. I would listen to him preach on strongholds, watch people come free through the preaching of the truth, and then try to free myself by using the procedures he described. Again my frustration, confusion, and disgust overwhelmed me. The reason for this was: I was trying to free myself instead of allowing God to do the job. I seldom find it as easy to apply spiritual truths as most other folks seem to. Even though Jack is my "resident professor," I am a very difficult pupil. God generally has to teach me in a slightly different manner! While I recognized strongholds, as Paul had discussed them in 2 Corinthians 10:3-6 I saw a great tree of bondage with all sorts of varied fruit on it. (We will discuss that more fully later.)

We have defined strongholds. Now let's talk about detecting them. Not every sin is a sign of a stronghold any more than every sneeze is a sign of a demon. But there are several telltale signs that indicate the presence of strongholds. Areas of continuous defeat may mark a stronghold. I had areas in my life where any victory I seemed to have was at best temporary. I might have gone a day or two, or even a week, but sooner or later things would tumble in around me regarding this particular area, and I would be back at ground zero. Some of these were jealousy, anger, hostility, resentment, suspicion, negativism, guilt, self-condemnation, self-pity, fear, ad infinitum and ad nauseum. Though I would confess these as sins and God would forgive me and refill me with His Spirit, I would soon come to defeat again.

These defeats occurred because of deep-rooted sins that were fixed in my inner life like tumors. My mind was filled with "stinkin' thinkin'."

Any time there are compulsions, fixations, or obsessions a stronghold may be suspicioned. Fear of storms, fears centering on obsessions, uncontrolled rage, compulsions to overeat, talk too much, watch too much television, or obsessions with cleanliness may indicate the presence of a stronghold. Fantasies that appear on the stage of the mind in day dreams, visions, or dreams suggest spiritual strongholds. I am convinced that many of the twentieth-century terms invented to describe varying kinds of mental illnesses, so-called, are nothing more than spiritual strongholds.

Continuing proneness to depression and repeated thoughts of suicide characterize the nature of strongholds. (This process began in my life after my first year of college.)

The presence of faults in our thinking, though obviously untrue yet stubbornly believed, are strongholds. (My brother had once told me in jest, "Sis, if we put your brains in a blue jay, it would fly backwards!" He meant no harm, but I came to believe that as gospel! My brother could do no wrong in my eyes, and I believed everything he said.) When there are such obviously unreasonable thought processes in one's mind the fault may be strongholds. Some of the most beautiful people I have ever seen believe that they are ugly, and no amount of convincing will change their minds.

When I began to perceive what the nature of a stronghold was, I also began to see the nature of my problems more clearly. I not only needed to be forgiven of sins, I needed to be delivered from strongholds.

As you read this chapter the matter of demonic influence is coming into the minds of many readers. This is a smoking battlefield in theological circles. The Christian world is not in agreement as to what influence a demon can exert on a Christian. There is no consensus about whether or not a Christian can "have" a demon. Someone was asked, "Can a Christian have a demon?" The answer was, "A Christian can have anything he wants!" Amen! I believe that a Christian can be influenced to the measure that he allows the enemy to do so. Paul warned, "Neither give place to the devil" (Eph. 4:27). This is not the place, and there is not the time to discuss fully this much-argued subject, but allow me to make some observations that might prove helpful now or later on. First, all evil, even the slightest critical thought, originated with the devil. So all wrong thinking and wrong acting, and all that goes with them, have come from the devil's headquarters. Where there are lies believed and practiced, the devil, his demons, and

their multiple influences are not far away. We will not
settle these long-discussed questions, but the fact remains that, whether the devil can read our thoughts,
demons can reside in a believer, or whether demons are
on, under, or around the Christian—*Christians are influenced at times by the powers of darkness in their
thinking and acting!* My private conviction is that, if a
stronghold is allowed to remain long in the believer's
life, the probabilities of serious demonic traffic will soon
be forthcoming. Regardless of what you choose to believe about this matter, please do not choose to disregard the danger of giving ground to Satan and allowing
his demons to unduly influence your life. It has happened to others, and it could happen to you. All the
more reason why we should get on with the business of
getting ourselves completely free from the clutches of
sin and Satan!

Before we leave the subject of strongholds I want to
discuss briefly something of their derivation—where
they begin. You will remember I was able to spot in my
memory precisely when the cycle of rejection began.
For some that is impossible since it was in the prenatal
stages. I believe that it was recorded deep within the
subconscious mind of a baby whether it was wanted or
unwanted. The seeds of rejection may be sown in the
very processes of conception. Love-conceived children
may prove to be very different children from lust-con-
ceived children. If a particular trauma accompanied the
birth experience a serious stronghold may show up in
later life.

I remember a doctor telling me of a woman who had

tried over twenty times to take her own life in her first twenty-one years! As research was carried out, it was determined that at her birth she was considered dead and laid on a cold table while doctors and nurses turned to the matter of keeping her seriously ill mother alive. When her mother was stabilized the team turned to the baby, who had already been considered dead, to discover signs of life. She was saved but was possessed with the thought, *I should be dead!* and repeatedly tried to accommodate her thoughts by trying to kill herself.

Strongholds of perversions may develop around only one episode. Homosexuality (a stronghold for sure!) may begin with one such experience as a child. Perversion forced upon a child or an adult may cause a severe stronghold later. Wrong disciplinary measures or abuse are apt to bring problems after awhile.

Many traits labeled "family traits" are strongholds that have been in the family for generations and are passed on in a continuous manner.

Strongholds can begin around a serious accident or a time of severe stress. America will be suffering the sad effects of the struggle in Vietnam for generations to come. There developed around the struggle a sense of corporate futility with a "no-win" mentality. The lads were not welcomed back home as heroes but were, in fact, rejected as villains. Hundreds of suicides and thousands of wrecked lives have resulted. And who can tell of the results even in yet-unborn generations?

Wrong emphases on valid spiritual truths may result in strongholds. The church has been scored as preaching a gospel of guilt, and in many cases the criticism is valid. Many have come out of strict Bible-believing homes and fundamental churches where more emphasis has been placed on the letter of the law than on the Spirit of God. The results are often strongholds of guilt, legalism, spiritual pride, or resignation and defeatism.

Later on I will discuss strongholds and how to destroy them. That will be a more pleasant chapter than this one has been!

You might spend a few moments to ponder and meditate about which parts of this chapter have been of particular interest to you and why. You may not be sure about all I have written. Don't worry. Take what strikes you as true and relevant, and lay the remainder on a shelf. It may prove helpful later on.

7

A Tree Grows in Barbara (The Tree of Bondage)

A strange title for a chapter! you may be thinking. What I am about to share with you is probably the most helpful revelation I have ever had in my own ongoing liberation. With that in mind I present it in a manner as nearly like I received it as possible.

When I began to view honestly my own bondage I envisioned it as a tree with roots, a trunk, limbs, and fruit. The subtitle of this chapter is "The Tree of Bondage." This put my bondage under a light of understanding as nothing had. Where was the tree growing? In my mind! We will later see the truth of the axiom, "As a man thinketh in his heart, so is he" (Prov. 23:7). I understood that what was in my mind was affecting the whole of my life. Therefore, it is not enough to acknowledge the existence of the tree of bondage but to examine its makeup, cut it down, and root it up, stopping its poisonous productivity.

I want you to understand I am aware that any illustration has its flaws and weaknesses, and this one is no exception. However, it has been of inestimable value to me and to hundreds wherever I have shared it. For these reasons I am giving it to you just as I received it from the Lord. Perhaps as with no other illustration I share, more people identify with this one. Since first receiving it I have seen more and more of its fruit which make up strongholds in the lives of human beings all over earth. The fruit on the limbs in the illustration are samples of an endless list of unwelcome fruit surrounding the deception of rejection. It is not without significance that the Bible, with all of the truths in it, is framed within the context of two trees, the tree of the knowledge of good and evil and the tree of life. After the tragedy of man's disobedience and subsequent fall, everything that happens to mankind is a result of fruit grown on one of those trees. What were those trees?

The simplest way of putting it is that the tree of the knowledge of good and evil is none other than the tree of self, and the tree of life is none other than Jesus Christ Himself. Any fruit that is false, unharmonious, destructive, or divisive is borne on the first tree; any fruit that is helpful, healthful, constructive, or life-giving issues from the latter.

May I suggest that you keep handy the illustration as you read this chapter? When I call attention to the roots on the tree take time to look at the illustration and examine the root structure. A basic understanding of the illustration will be necessary to your maximum benefit from this particular study. I will remind you from time to time to refer to the illustration. For your information the illustration of the Tree of Bondage is found on page 93.

Let's start at ground level, a good place to start, don't

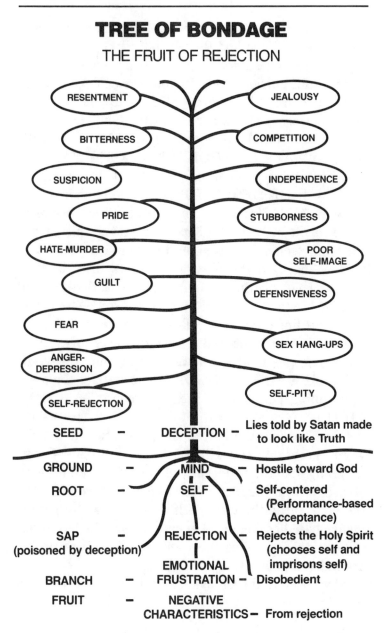

TREE OF BONDAGE
THE FRUIT OF REJECTION

RESENTMENT

JEALOUSY

BITTERNESS

COMPETITION

SUSPICION

INDEPENDENCE

PRIDE

STUBBORNESS

HATE-MURDER

POOR SELF-IMAGE

GUILT

DEFENSIVENESS

FEAR

SEX HANG-UPS

ANGER-DEPRESSION

SELF-PITY

SELF-REJECTION

SEED	– DECEPTION –	Lies told by Satan made to look like Truth
GROUND	– MIND –	Hostile toward God
ROOT	– SELF –	Self-centered (Performance-based Acceptance)
SAP (poisoned by deception)	– REJECTION –	Rejects the Holy Spirit (chooses self and imprisons self)
BRANCH	– EMOTIONAL FRUSTRATION –	Disobedient
FRUIT	– NEGATIVE CHARACTERISTICS –	From rejection

you think? Please refer to the illustration, ground level, left side where you find the word "SEED." Every tree, regardless of size, kind, or age, has had a beginning with a seed, soil, nutrients, etc. In your view of the illustration move from the word "SEED" to the center at ground level and the word "DECEPTION." On toward the right at ground level is the phrase "LIES TOLD BY SATAN MADE TO LOOK LIKE TRUTH." So there you have the beginning of the Tree of Bondage, the SEED which is DECEPTION sown by Satan as LIES. Do you see it? If not, hold up until the light begins to come through. Don't let Satan rob you of this part of the truth which God is going to use to set you free!

Now, back to the illustration. Let's drop back to ground level on the left and look beneath the word "SEED" to the word "GROUND" (or soil). Moving on a straight line across you will find the word "MIND." The soil in which the seed is sown by the enemy is none other than the mind. On across you will find the words "HOSTILE TOWARD GOD." The state of the mind in its unregenerate and unrenewed condition is HOSTILITY.

Now, back to the left on the illustration under the word "ground." You will see the word "root." Corresponding to in the middle as you move from left to right, you see within the root system the word "self." And to the far right is the term "self-centered" with "performance-based acceptance" in parentheses. This is rather self-explanatory since the root of the problem forms around the network of "self" problems.

Now, back to the left again and the word "SAP." Do

you see it? Sap is the "stuff" of life in the tree that determines the nature of the fruit. On a straight line across, at center, you see the word "REJECTION." Rejection is the essence of the whole Tree of Bondage from root to fruit. The nature of rejection is inherent in the word itself. On across on a straight line are the words "REJECTS THE HOLY SPIRIT." In reality this Tree of Bondage is an unwelcomed intruder, a life foreign to that of God, a system set against truth. Its fruit tends to poison the whole system.

Look to the last two lines at the bottom of the illustration. These will prepare us to go "above ground" and observe the symptoms of our bondage as we view the fruit. A common mistake that is made in this matter of seeking liberation is that of treating the symptoms without treating the source. In line with our present illustration the better terms here are "treating the fruit without treating the root." For that reason I don't want you to leave the root structure until we have a basic understanding of its nature. On the BRANCHES are carried the fruit. From deception grows rejection which moves through the limbs (EMOTIONAL FRUSTRATION) to bear the deadly fruit. Disobedience results.

The bottom line of the illustration simply suggests that the FRUIT is THE NEGATIVE CHARACTERISTICS which issue from rejection.

Now, let's summarize what we have learned from "ground level" and below. The Tree of Bondage is rooted around self rather than God, as was the Tree of the Knowledge of Good and Evil. In fact, it might be said that for all practical purposes the Tree of Bondage as we have described it is a modern-day Tree of the Knowledge of Good and Evil. The ground, or soil, is the mind which in its unregenerate and unrenewed state is hostile to God. The tap root, as it were, is none other than this SELF as man's identity separated from God. The SAP which is basically REJECTION pervades the whole tree from root to fruit with its essence.

The BRANCHES are the pipelines from the root system through the trunk to the FRUIT. Each of these items I call FRUIT are the results of disobedience. All you or I or the world ever sees of this Tree of Bondage is its FRUIT. The seed, soil, sap, and branches are quite invisible but are most vital to the understanding of the fruit.

Before we go "above ground" in our illustration let me interject another facet of my testimony. Because I did not understand my true identity in Christ I thought that these diabolical fruits I was bearing marked me as a wicked person. I did not see that I was new while there remained in me roots that, left alone, would continue to bear fruit. So, at best, it was left for me to "pick the fruit" and destroy them, praying for crop failure in the future. But I seldom had such a desired "crop failure" in the production of the Tree of Bondage! The atmosphere in which that tree grows (the world) seems to be filled with all that is conducive to maximum productivity! And as long as my mind was deceived into believing what the world system taught, the soil of my mind remained fertile indeed.

Now we go to "above ground." We will start up the tree on the left side from bottom to top. I will name the

FRUIT, seek to define it, share a Scriptural reference in most instances, and then add a personal testimony. Ready? Here we go!

Self-Rejection

Since the very essence of the life of the Tree of Bondage is rejection it may be expected that this is the primary fruit. There is a quality of rejection in every individual fruit that will be mentioned. The church has not been very clear as to what we are to do without "selves." Are we to resist, flee, fight, hate, or love self? Jesus never taught us to reject our *new selves,* who we are in Christ. We are to "put off the *old man* with his affections and lusts" (Eph. 4:22). The "old man" means what we were BC (Before Christ).

I had not learned the difference between the old man and the new man. I thought that because the old fruit remained, surely the old man remained. Somewhere in me, so I thought, the new man lay languishing in prison with little possibility of escaping. All I knew to do was to fight this old man with all my might. You can see the reason why my own mind was the scene of a "civil war" with no truce.

Anger and Depression

Jack asked me why I put these two together since they are both such problems in themselves. I will try to answer that question since it may reflect what many of you will be asking. Many Christian leaders who talk and write about anger and depression believe they are tied together, whether or not the person victimized by them understands the logistics of them. Among these are Tim LaHaye and Charles Solomon. Solomon has expressed that depression is really at heart an "internal temper tantrum." The first time I heard him personally make that statement I wanted to jump up and hit him with my fist. But, thank God, I merely sat there and fumed, not realizing at the time that my own inner feelings were proof that he was right!

I was angry, and I had to admit it. I was as mad as the proverbial "wet hen," mad at myself, mad at God, mad at Jack, mad at my fellow-workers and associates, mad at my circumstances, and mad at anything or anyone else who happened to stand in my way. I tried to mask it, hide it, or perform cosmetic surgery on my anger. But I am not one to hide my feelings very well. I was like a volcano on the inside, waiting to erupt and not wanting to admit that I was ultimately angry with God because I was not getting MY way!

Tim LaHaye says in his book *How to Win Over Depression,* "The first step in the chain reaction producing depression is anger. Don't be surprised that you involuntarily reject such a proposal. I have consistently observed that most depressed persons cannot and do not think of themselves as angry people."[1] (Was he right about me!) So, I have placed them together in our consideration because they go together. You seldom, if ever, see one without the other. Most every depressed person is angry, and most every angry person is de-

pressed. Let us observe some Scriptures on the subject
of anger:

> He who is angry dealeth foolishly, and a man of
> wicked intentions is hated (Prov. 14:17).
> Make no friendship with an angry man, and with
> a furious man do not go lest you learn his ways
> and set a snare for your soul (Prov. 22:24-25).
> An angry man stirreth up strife, and a furious man
> abounds in transgression (Prov. 29:22).

For a biblical illustration on the subject of depression
read the record of Elijah in the experience Jack calls
"The Juniper Tree Syndrome" or "Elijah's Post-Carmel
Letdown." This story is found in 1 Kings 19. Interest-
ingly enough you will find many of the fruits mentioned
in this chapter in Elijah's life during that experience.
Take the time to see how many of them you can detect.

Fear

Fear is a common ingredient in rejection. It carries
with it an expectation of more rejection and is a self-
fulfilling feature in itself.

My own life was laden with fear. Fear of being left.
Fear of being late. Fear of being hurt again. Fear of
having my head covered. Fear of more rejection. I think
at times I created fears that as yet had not been invented. I am told there are upwards of a hundred differing
phobias and new ones being invested with frequency as
life on earth complicates.

Fear and anxiety are somewhat synonymous. I was

anxious that I might fail again and that was what fueled my PBA.

While it is commonly held that the opposite of fear is courage I believe that the opposite of fear is *love*. I cannot fear what or whom I love, and I cannot love what or whom I fear. The Bible says, "There is no fear in love; but perfect love casteth out fear; because fear hath torment" (1 John 4:18). I tried to pass over the crystal-clear teachings of the Word of God to "fear not," and to "put on the whole armour of God, that ye may be able to stand in the evil day." But I was filled with fear. Somehow I had never claimed John 16:24, "Hitherto have ye asked nothing in my name: ask, and ye shall receive, that your joy may be full." Neither had I appropriated John 14:17, "Peace I leave with you, my peace give I unto you; not as the world giveth, give I unto you. Let not your heart be troubled, neither let it be afraid" (John 14:27)

My mind now travels back to those many nights when mother worked the graveyard shift from eleven o'clock in the evening until seven o'clock in the morning. I was all alone with my many and multiplying fears. I imagined everything. The old Cornish litany had it, "Ghouls and ghosties, and fearsome creatures, and things that go bump in the night."

No wonder that over and over again Jesus spoke reassuringly to his disciples, "Fear not!"

Guilt

Guilt is generally found in the cluster of the fruit of rejection. We are dealing here with the "false" brand of guilt. It is genuine guilt that drives the sinner to conviction, repentance, faith, and regeneration. It is false guilt that prevents the person who has been accepted in Christ from accepting that acceptance.

I had so much imagined or false guilt that I was always expecting to be punished for whatever I had done.

Jack and I still joke about my behavior when I see a policeman or a traffic cop. I respond in my mind with the following thought process: *Oh-oh, what have I done now? He has come to take me. I knew that I would eventually be found out!* I was guilt looking for punishment. I will never forget the time Jack and I were vacationing in Cancun. We were walking up the road, and a policeman drove toward us slowly. Impulsively I walked toward the car and all but held out my hands for him to put the handcuffs on me, compulsively certain that here in this out-of-the-way place in the world my sins had finally caught up with me. Now, isn't that silly? Yes, but not all that much fun to live with!

Now the truth about guilt is that Jesus bore it all on Calvary. When we accept His death as ours, the payment for sin is immediately and permanently completed. Paul expressed it well when he declared, "There is therefore no condemnation [guilt] to them who are in Christ Jesus . . ." (Rom. 8:1).

Hate/Murder

I linked anger with depression by means of an "and."
I link hate and murder with a slash line because they are
connected more closely than associates. They are Sia-
mese twins that are forever inseparable. You cannot
have one without the other within the emotions. When
you hate someone enough to condemn them verbally,
the only difference between that and murder is in degree
and not in kind. Hate contains the corrupt seeds of
murder. Jesus made it clear that if one is hateful toward
another, he is mentally guilty of murder, as though he
had committed a homocide.

"You have heard it said to those of old, 'You shall not
murder.' and whoever murders shall be in danger of the
judgment. But I say to you that whosoever is angry with
his brother without a cause shall be in danger of the
judgment." (Matt. 5:21-22, NASB)

Before the Lord began my liberation process I hated
myself and had feelings of hatred toward everyone else.
I was sure of almost everything and hated those who
would have the audacity to disagree with me. I was sure
of things of which I knew absolutely nothing! In my
mind, I suppose, I had to be right in order to prove
myself so I would not be rejected. In the very attempt
to insure myself against rejection I was all but guaran-
teeing it! Actually when we hate, the venom of murder
is poured into our internal systems, thus poisoning all
of life. It was so with me.

Pride

While pride or self-centeredness is a root, it is also a fruit on the Tree of Bondage. However you spell it or pronounce it, backwards or forwards, it has an "I" right in the middle! This is the feeling that assumes "I am the center of the universe!" "Everything revolves around me"! I was diagnosed by a dear friend as having a "global-responsibility syndrome." This is but another expression of pride. I secretly felt and ultimately said that if I had the attention of the whole world as a first-grade classroom, as its teacher, I could settle the world's woes presently! I honestly felt this to be true. Such unmitigated egotism and unvarnished pride!

The word appropriately says, "Pride goeth before destruction, and a haughty spirit before a fall" (Prov. 16:18). It certainly proved so in my case and I guarantee you, it will be so in your life!

Suspicion

I think I am going to have a headache examining all this distasteful fruit! But stay with me, and we will soon take a break!

Rejection is filled with distrust which lays a sound foundation for suspicion. I took on suspicion rather naturally since Mother was filled with it. Because she was so often mistreated she had trouble trusting anyone. I grew up in an atmosphere of suspicion with both Mother and Daddy. Daddy accused mother of the very sins he was practicing!

I didn't trust my parents, my husband, my children, or God. Can you imagine that I didn't trust my own husband? He has always proved to be completely trustworthy. I know that now, but at the time my imaginations were, oh, so real. He never would have done anything to betray my trust but because of all the garbage and trash I had in my mind, he was the object of my constant suspicion. I imagined all sorts of things, including his being involved with other women. The fact that I had transferred the actions of my father to Jack caused me merely to conclude that Jack would surely engage in the same kind of relationships. It may be a woman reading these words is having the same suspicions for essentially the same reasons. I should warn you: many husbands so suspicioned have reacted so drastically as to actually go ahead with such relationships of which they had been previously accused.

A final word about suspicion—*stop it right now!* You willed to be suspicious—*now will to stop it!*

Bitterness

Have you ever been bitter, even for a little while? It's terrible. Can you imagine that I wallowed in it for years? I felt bitterness for being born, bitterness for being rejected, bitterness for having to live, bitterness for being too cowardly to kill myself, and bitterness for even thinking of doing so.

I must have felt like Job when he cried, "Let the day perish on which I was to be born, And the night which said, 'A boy is conceived.' May that day be darkness;

Let not God above care for it. Nor light shine on it"
(Job 3:3-4, NASB). Now that is bitterness!—to pray for
retroactive birth-control! But that is about how bitter I
was. Praise the Lord, I can laugh about it now!

Resentment

I was tempted to put bitterness and resentment
together but treat them separately because they seem to
describe two different stages on the keyboard of our
emotions. Feelings of resentment given expressions may
grow into a rigid bitterness. My testimony is proof of
this fact. My resentment was aroused with anyone who
got in my way, even those I loved the most and who
loved me! I saw my own condition reflected in the attitude and actions of the elder brother in the story of the
prodigal son. I was full of resentment, mad at my sur-
roundings, and lashing out at anyone around me.

My own resentment made me physically ill. I had a
compulsion to have something taken out of me. In the
process of three operations the doctor removed about
everything in me that could be removed without ending
my life. But somehow he never removed bitterness and
resentment in that manner. All three operations were
"major" surgeries. When I asked the doctor the difference between "major" and "minor" surgery he replied,
"Major surgery is when I have it. Minor surgery is when
you have it." Clever.

Break time! Let's do something light for a change and
relieve ourselves of this burden of "bad fruit inspec-

tion"! I will take up the other side of the Tree of Bondage in the next chapter.

NOTE
1. Tim LaHaye, *How to Win Over Depression* (Grands Rapids, MI: Zondervan Publishing House, 1974), p. 85.

8

The Tree of Bondage . . . More Rotten Fruit

Now that you have had a break from inspecting the fruit on the "terrible tree," let's continue. Put a marker on page 93 where the illustration of The Tree of Bondage is located. We ended the last chapter with the topmost fruit on the left side of the tree—resentment. We will move downward on the right side of the tree.

Jealousy

I have no idea what is on your tree, but this fruit was obvious on mine. Jealousy was a way of life with me. When one is unsure of a position held and is uncertain about the ability to hold that position, jealousy is aroused. That was Barbara! Jealousy has been defined as fear of someone else taking away from us what we hold to be ours.

Go along on my journey with jealousy. I seemed to have learned jealousy, as I learned much else, from my family. Mother was jealous of Daddy and with good reason! I not only learned jealousy from her but developed a good case of my own as I saw other women not

only replace my mother—but replace me. My first stepmother was only four years older than I! So you can
imagine I was filled with jealousy before I knew the
meaning of the term.

It was almost predictable that I carry this jealousy
into my marriage with Jack. My insecurity dictated a
fear that I would lose what was dearest to me.

It will be worth the space and time to tell you of the
night my jealousy was exposed in all its hellish fury, the
result being the facing of it and dealing with it. Our
church had been in an time of spiritual awakening and
had developed a ministry among Air Force pilots from
South Vietnam, Thailand, Cambodia, Korea, and Laos.
We had found in this group a fertile mission field, had
led many of them to Christ, and had the privilege of
ministering to them in Christian growth.

This particular night the church members had been
invited to the pilots' graduation, after which they would
return to their homelands to share the Gospel with their
own people. Included in their group were many others
who had not accepted Christ. It would be another night
of opportunities to present Jesus. When we arrived at
the Air Force base, most of our church staff was already
there. Our associate pastor was already talking to one
of the foreign students.

As soon as he saw Jack he beckoned him to come
over and speak with the young man further about receiving Christ. At that moment "old green eyes" raised
its ugly head. When I should have been concerned and
praying for Jack I was jealous of his time and his gift
of winning people to Jesus. To add sin to sin I said to

myself, *I'll show him (Jack). I'll find me someone to witness to and win them to Christ.* Can you imagine reasoning like that? There I was witnessing up a storm with jealousy filling my mind! It became even worse.

The person I was witnessing to began to respond favorably. The Holy Spirit was using me despite myself. I was so engrossed with my witnessing experience I almost forgot my aggravation and jealousy. I called two of the secretaries over to help me witness to this man. When he turned his attentions to them instead of me those feelings of jealousy returned. I began to feel anxious and competitive once more. Yes, I am aware that this kind of flip-flop seems to border on the insane. But see, both you and I know that jealousy does not behave along the lines of the sensible or the sane. Well, before long I had dropped into my little cubbyhole of rejection and began to withdraw. Amid communicating the Gospel I became uncommunicative.

By the time the evening was over I had a huge episode of rejection going, and Jack was well aware of it as usual. On the way home he asked me what the problem was, and I lashed out with more rejection. The fight (verbally) was on. Suddenly we both became aware that our marriage had reached an impasse, and we were totally unable to communicate. We were so desperate that, instead of going on home, we drove by the church and went in the darkened auditorium for prayer at the altar. It probably didn't do much good, since we were angry when we prayed, but we had made a move in the right direction. The evening continued with hurting words, attacks, and counterattacks.

The result was that, after we had emptied our verbal cannons at each other with reactions becoming more and more serious, there were no more words, only searing and unrelieved anger and frustration as a hundred times before. But this time there was something that had not existed before, fear, fear that we had crossed the line of "no return," fear that something had snapped in our marriage which not be repairable, and fear that love may have been slaughtered on the altar of our own selfishness. I will not go into the details of the evening, but I will tell you that was the evening when, for the first time after seventeen years of marriage, we submitted our selfish wills to each other, and jealousy was dealt a mortal blow. That could have happened only with the exposure of the unmasked evil of jealousy at the party that night.

Competition

You saw in my jealousy story how competition entered in. Well, since all the world was a stage to Barbara, I had to compete. Lights! Camera! Action! I was in competition with everybody, including my own husband. It was the only way I had learned to measure the success of my performance. I not only sought to outdo my rivals—I came to hate them.

I did not grow up in church so I had not developed some of the ecclesiastical "graces." I did not sing. I did not play the piano. I began to perceive Jack as my competition. While the Bible teaches that woman was to complete man, I, bent on competition, was out to *finish* him!

It became a joking matter with us. A pulpit committee would talk to Jack and me. Invariably a member of the committee would ask me, "Can you play the piano?" I would then answer, "No, but Jack can." One would then ask, "Do you sing?" I would answer, "No, but Jack does!" Then they would look at me with that "what-do-you-do?" look, and I would reply, "By the way, I do a wonderful 'soft-shoe' routine!" End of interview! (I am wondering now if that might be the reason Jack pastored only two churches in twenty years!)

Competition is an ingredient the marriage can do without. We may *complete or compete*—but not both!

Independence

The matter of independence is expressly forbidden in the Bible; in fact, it is an impossibility. "No man lives to himself and no man dies to himself. For if we live, we live to the Lord; and if we die, we die to the Lord. Therefore whether we live or die, we are the Lord's" (Rom. 14:7-8). Rejection seems to have a habit of flaunting independence while crying for acceptance. Jack uses a country saying, "As independent as a hog on ice." I had heard it used many times before he explained it one day. A hog (or pig) on ice is so bent on trying to stay erect it will thrash its legs so violently that anyone trying to help is apt to be hurt. Score one for the hogs—and Barbara!

Stubbornness

Could all of this fruit have been on my tree? Afraid so! A good friend of ours specialized in euphemisms. He had a gem for every occasion and every person. He would say of a person with an exceptionally strong will, "He's so stubborn, if his head itched, he'd scratch his foot!" I was much like the little boy whose mother told him to sit on the front seat of the car since an accident might occur, and he would be hurt. He reluctantly sat down but was heard to mutter, "I'm sitting down on the outside, but I'm standing up on the inside!"

I might add here in my defense (I have really let down my defenses, haven't I?) that these qualities do have a positive side when the Holy Spirit gets hold of us. My stubbornness, for instance, in its sanctified state, has saved me from error of all kinds on many occasions. But as a fruit on the Tree of Bondage it is quite lacking in redeeming features!

Poor Self-Image

This fruit goes along with all the other currupt fruit on the tree. Much of our mental anguish in life stems from a poor self-image. I have done it all to win my own approval only to find that I cannot do enough in the flesh to redeem my mistaken identity. To my delight I am in the process of discovering that God has another image of me in His mind. He sees me IN CHRIST and approves of me on that basis. You will perhaps see more welcome light on this much-discussed subject when we come to talk in a later chapter about our identity in Christ and its affect on our rejection.

Defensiveness

An inevitable outgrowth of rejection is defensiveness. It goes hand in hand with the lack of trust and performance-based acceptance. On the one hand I found myself acting in such a way as to invite rejection, and then would turn around and defend myself against the real and anticipated reactions. Once a friend approached me and asked me, "Well, are you going to hug me or hit me today?" My reply was, "I haven't decided yet!" You see, when I was in a rejection episode I wanted to strike out at something or someone, and that's exactly what I did with my attitudes and words. When I was normal (not in rejection) I was loving and thoughtful. I was almost like a Jekyll-and-Hyde personality.

When a person is prone to defensiveness every word is viewed as a suspicioned personal attack. Many times when Jack would make a statement I would react with unreasoned suspicion ask say rather hatefully, "Just what did you mean by that?" Sometimes someone would say "Hello" to me, and I would want to question their tone and intent and want to ask again, "What did you mean by that?"

I might add at this point: it is tiring to live on the defensive. I know. I could have won the award as "Most Defensive Person of the Year." Everyone was suspect in my mind, and this would necessitate my taking a defensive stance. I was defensive not only of myself but my family, my church, my friends, and all else in which I had personal interest.

Sex Hang-ups

As I promised—no secrets! OK? My preference would have been to leave out this material, but because it was part of the whole picture, and because I know there are those among you who can relate, here goes!

In the computer of my mind sex was everything but beautiful. It was dirty, tawdry, and caused disharmony, and all this brought guilt, anger, hostility, and division. I saw sex at its worst and never at its God-intended best. Sexual episodes were taking place all around me, resulting in divorce and further rejection.

So you can see it was quite natural that I would lug into my marriage with Jack the heavy baggage of multiple sex hang-ups.

I looked upon sex as a duty at best and a very unenjoyable one at worst. This ushered in more guilt, suspicion, and fear. Now that I am experiencing liberation in this area, I have given up my stage and performance, and thus I don't have to *perform* in the bed. And while we are on this point, honesty dictates that Barbara step on a soapbox for a moment. One of the profound unaddressed tragedies of divorce lies in this area of sex hang-ups in the lives of the children caught in divorce. Most of them have seen adultery take place and have reacted against the whole sexual scene.

They may have seen or been the victims of sexual abuse, perversion, or at best the exercise of sex in the wrong ways. Then they may become open prey to every sexual hang-up imaginable. What I am saying, then, to you adults who have "had it" with each other, and are considering divorce as the only alternative, *Stop and think of your children and their yet-unborn children and choose for their well-being over your present whims and feelings! Tough it out! Let up on each other! Every married couple has experienced most of what you are experiencing. Take each other off probation and performance-based acceptance.*

As I step down off my soapbox it might help you if I confess that Jack and I have had our moments when we wondered if we were going to make it. We talk about it now by joking facetiously, "Divorce? Never! Murder? Perhaps!"

Before we leave this touchy subject let me be honest with you about another point. This will stand to help both men and women. It is something Jack and I have come to understand with tremendous benefit. A man tends to view sex as a single, isolated episode. A woman looks upon it as a meaningful part of the whole relationship. To the man the marriage bed is quite unrelated to the house, the job, the events of the day or week, or the attention he has withheld or given his wife in the past. But with the woman all sorts of thought processes escort her to the marriage bed. When her husband touches her, floodlights come on, illuminating past neglects, affections forgotten, and words spoken in harshness without apology. She thinks of chores undone around the house and thinks his only motive surely must be to have his own lusts satisfied and hurry back to his business. And now: a commercial! Why don't you, husband, pick up a copy of Jack's book *What Every Husband Should Know*? I say this part in jest and part in all seriousness, "Most of what he has written in the book, he learned from me!" (You see, the Lord and I have done a good job with Jack!)

Amid this heavy stuff let me remind you that with liberation there is not the loss of the genuine but the cleansing of the product. Spirit-filled sex is one of the greatest pleasures on the face of the earth.

Self-Pity

This is only one of the ills among many that are self-related. You will remember in the previous chapter that we began with self-rejection. We are ending this with self-pity. While they seem at opposite ends of the emotional spectrum they seem always to go together. One demands the other. We have declared that the Tree of Bondage is supported by the tap root of *self* and could name a dozen self-related fruits growing on the tree. Self-pity is a means of getting attention, winning a point, and may become passive hostility.

Until God began to straighten out the frazzles and tangles of my personality I was always walking in self-pity, having a "pity-party" or sitting on the "pity-pot-ty"! Poor me! The whole world is set against me! I sounded like the older son in the story of the prodigal. "Lo, these many years do I serve thee, and have never at any time transgressed thy commandment; and yet thou never gavest me a kid that I might make merry with my friends" (Luke 15:29). I was like that much of the time, wallowing in self-pity like a pig rolls in the mud.

I came to realize that self-pity dictates that self is the center around which the whole world revolves. With self-pity there could be no genuine ministry, no devoted service, and no sense of victory. It assumes that, "I am my keeper, my only defense."

Praise the Lord, I do not have to continue in this "slough of despond." Neither do you!

I am glad to see this chapter come to and end. And you and I will be glad to see this terrible Tree of Bondage dismantled, chopped down, neutralized, and become a faint memory in the light of His victory! In the coming chapter this will be our focus.

9
Destroying Strongholds . . .
A Soul Set Free

I have sought to show you how I perceived my own bondage as a massive tree with multiple fruit. It was more than a matter of sin, and even more than a static condition. My bondage was like that tree which kept on producing its fruit. To put it in other words: it was a factory that kept on producing its varying lines of woeful wares. In this chapter we are going to talk about how God began to uproot the terrible tree of bondage, tear down the strongholds, and set my soul free.

But before we come to discuss destroying those strongholds I want you to view the illustration of our basic makeup on page *120*. You will notice that it is made up of three concentric circles. The outer circle represents the BODY, the next circle inward stands for the SOUL, and the last circle inside symbolizes the SPIRIT.

Now, I realize there is an age-old discussion about whether man is a two-part or a three-part being. Those who believe that man is simply BODY and SPIRIT (or SOUL) have some questions to answer about a couple of biblical passages regarding the difference in soul and

SOUL SET FREE

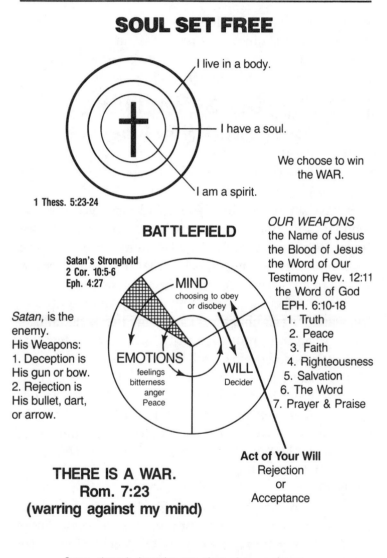

I live in a body.

I have a soul.

We choose to win
the WAR.

I am a spirit.

1 Thess. 5:23-24

BATTLEFIELD

OUR WEAPONS
the Name of Jesus
the Blood of Jesus
the Word of Our
Testimony Rev. 12:11
the Word of God
EPH. 6:10-18
1. Truth
2. Peace
3. Faith
4. Righteousness
5. Salvation
6. The Word
7. Prayer & Praise

Satan's Stronghold
2 Cor. 10:5-6
Eph. 4:27

MIND
choosing to obey
or disobey

Satan, is the
enemy.
His Weapons:
1. Deception is
His gun or bow.
2. Rejection is
His bullet, dart,
or arrow.

EMOTIONS
feelings
bitterness
anger
Peace

WILL
Decider

Act of Your Will
Rejection
or
Acceptance

THERE IS A WAR.
Rom. 7:23
(warring against my mind)

Satan—through deception gets place when we choose
to believe his lies. He will make a lie look like the Truth.

We must choose to believe the truth, the Word of God,
and what it says. Claim and Obey 2 Cor. 10:4-6; 2 Cor. 5:17.

spirit. For instance in Hebrews 4:12 we read, "For the Word of God is quick and powerful, and sharper than a two-edged sword, piercing even to the *dividing asunder of soul and spirit,* and of the joints and marrow, and is a discerner of the thoughts and intents of the heart." It is apparent here that the author certainly recognized the existence of the spirit separate from the body. Then in one of my favorite passages, 1 Thessalonians 5:23-24, we see, "And the very God of peace sanctify you wholly; and I pray God your *whole spirit, soul, and body* be preserved blameless unto the coming of our Lord Jesus Christ. Faithful is he that calleth you, who will also do it." Again here is the evident supposition that there are three parts to our basic makeup—BODY, SOUL, AND SPIRIT.

Now, look again at the illustration. It is correct to say, "I live in a BODY." The body is not I, but where I live. It is my temporary home, my means of mobility, the entity that relates me to physical reality. It is, as one of our friends puts it, simply our "earth suit."

While I *live* in a BODY, I *have* a SOUL. My soul is made up of my mind (my thinking part), my emotions (my feeling part), and my will (my deciding part). You see the soul spotlighted in the next part of the illustration. Take a moment to look back at the illustration. (Stay close to it throughout this chapter for maximum understanding.) My SOUL relates me as an identity to others around me. We will come back to this illustration as we talk of breaking the bondage later on.

So I *live* in a BODY; I *have* a SOUL; but I *am* a SPIRIT. In my essential, authentic, eternal identity I

AM A SPIRIT. When I was saved my SPIRIT was made one with God's Spirit. I came alive spiritually, was born again, and began to be lived in by God's Spirit. I became a new creature in the realm of the SPIRIT. I am, then, perfected in the SPIRIT part of me.

Now, where the "rub" comes is that I still live in the same BODY and still have the same SOUL. So I, as a SPIRIT, am stuck with an unredeemed body and an unrenewed mind with problems in the realm of the emotions and will. So in identifying the soul we have located the battlefield. We have lived, up to the time of our salvation experience, with a mind filled with wrong beliefs, emotions filled with harmful feelings, and wills given to destructive behavior. And all this is spelled B-O-N-D-A-G-E! And from it we need to be set free. What a wonderful declaration Jesus makes in John 8:31-32, "If you continue in my word then are ye my disciples indeed. And ye shall know the truth, and the truth shall make you free." So there is blessed "relief" to the "rub" of our bondage. We should not leave the John 8 passage without reading a later verse (36) which goes, "If the Son shall make you free, ye shall be free indeed." So the Word (written) and the Word (Living, which is Christ) combine to make us *free!*

I am living proof of the power of the written Word of God to change a life. I have found it indeed to be true based on these words from Scripture, "For they are life to those that find them, and health to all their flesh" (Prov. 4:22). My Lord Jesus has used His power through the written words of Scripture to begin in me an exciting adventure of liberation!

Now, the passage I want to focus on, and with which I will be dealing most of this chapter, is found in 2 Corinthians 10:3-6. I want every word of it before you, and be prepared to return to it again and again. You could simplify the situation by taking the time right now to memorize it. I can guarantee you that it will prove an eternally beneficial investment of your time and effort. Take a memorization break! The passage is immediately below:

> For though we walk in the flesh, we do not war after the flesh. For the weapons of our warfare are not carnal, but mighty through God to the pulling down of strongholds; casting down imaginations, and every high thing that exalteth against the knowledge of God, and bringing into captivity every thought to the obedience of Christ; and having in a readiness to revenge all disobedience, when your obedience is fulfilled" (2 Cor. 10:3-6)

Of all the words of Scripture that God is using in my liberation, this passage is proving to be the most powerful! In fact, I want to walk you through it as the Lord first carried me through it.

Let's return now to the part of the illustration labeled the BATTLEFIELD or the circle divided into three parts: the MIND, the EMOTIONS, and the WILL. The shaded section of the mind I have labeled STRONGHOLDS. The arrow moving from the mind into the emotions represents the influence of the mind's thinking on the emotions. You might remember the little adage, "Wrong beliefs cause harmful emotions," or, "Misbeliefs cause misfeelings." The arrow of influence from the mind through the emotions ultimately affects the WILL which determines the nature of our behavior. So we may complete the adage, *"Misbeliefs* cause *misfeelings* which, in turn, cause *misbehavior."*

Examine the illustration again on page 120. At the center of the page on the left you will read, "Satan is the enemy." His *weapon* (gun or bow) is DECEPTION, and his *ammunition* (bullets, darts, or arrows) is REJECTION. It should be kept in mind that, while the enemy is real, he is less obvious than the world system which surrounds us and the flesh which pervades us. I have asserted that THERE IS A WAR. Paul declared it in Romans 7:23, "But I see another law in my members, warring against the law of my mind, and bringing me into captivity to the law of sin which is in my members."

Now, the walk-through of 2 Corinthians 10:3-6. Before Jesus came into my life I was all flesh. Now the warfare is in the realm of the spirit. Any warfare calls for weapons. In the war the weapons of the flesh will not do. Only spiritual weapons will prove destructive to spiritual strongholds. What are our weapons?

You see a suggested list of them to the right of center in the illustration. They are listed under the Scripture in Ephesians 6:10-18. Take time to read that passage which gives us an overview of our war. Included in this list of weapons are the Name of Jesus, the Word of God, the blood of Jesus, the word of our testimony, and our commitment to die, if necessary. These last three weapons are mentioned in Revelation 12:11, "And they overcame him [the devil] by the blood of the Lamb, and by the word of their testimony; and they loved not their lives unto the death." Our 2 Corinthians 10 passage asserts that our weapons are not carnal but MIGHTY THROUGH GOD. These weapons are able, adequate, and MIGHTY!

As we walk through this passage let us imagine we are also walking through the realms of our minds, emotions, and wills. We are talking about the "pulling down of strongholds" in the mind. The direction of influence, with strongholds influencing the mind, seems to move clockwise through the emotions to wrongly affect the will. As strongholds are pulled down we can choose with an unhindered will to do right. The emotions may be allowed to follow naturally. As you feature the weapons God is going to use for your liberation, let me suggest a visualization you might want to use. I will, in fact, suggest one of several from which you may choose.

Jack loves to share that he visualizes the weapons as a mighty bulldozer with a gigantic blade as wide as the regions of our minds. That bulldozer is none other than the weapons exercised in the mighty power of God. That visualization is not exactly a woman's way of thinking. (But for a man it is appropriate.) I don't think in those categories. One lady, after hearing about strongholds, visualized them all on a piece of paper, and in her mind flushed them down the commode. Some plumbing problem that might cause! For me the best illustration has proved to be that of a gigantic chalkboard framed in concrete or bricks. This may sound weird to you, but in my mind I put on that chalkboard all those memories of my mess of strongholds. I then featured that God had handed me a gigantic eraser which represented the blood of Jesus which I used to erase the chalkboard. I watched them vanish as strongholds or points of bondage in my mind.

This is what God does with our sins by the blood of Jesus. He removes them, remits them, erases them. So I erased those lousy, rotten sins (strongholds) one by one. And I wrote across that imaginary chalkboard the words, "If we confess our sins, he is faithful and just to forgive us our sins, and to cleanse us from all unrighteousness" (1 John 1:9). I have relived this experience again and again as necessary.

I don't want to confuse you with too many visualizations, but let me suggest another that has been of considerable benefit to me. One of those strongholds kept coming back to my mind again and again. It was like garbage I kept allowing to come into my mind. I prayed to the Lord and asked Him what to do with this garbage. He seemed to instruct me: bundle this trash up like the garbage it is and ready it for the "garbage pickup." So in my mind I did exactly that. In my imagination I put the trash in a garbage sack, tied it tightly, and took it to the garbage pickup point. Garbage, treated like garbage, goes where garbage ought to go. If you treat it like flowers and put it in a vase on the mantle, problems develop. If you treat it like delicious fruit and serve it for supper further complications develop. But when the truck comes by for the garbage it goes who knows where, and who cares? The fact is, it is gone! I have the feeling that, in this case, it is gone as far as the

East is from the West, as David described our transgressions being removed (see Ps. 103:12). Then I can lay claim to Philippians 3:13-14: "Brethren, I count not myself to have apprehended: but this one thing I do, *forgetting those things which are behind,* and reaching forth unto those which are before, I press toward the mark for the prize of the high calling of God in Christ Jesus."

We are still walking. Remember? Don't become weary in the walk. In 2 Corinthians 10:4-5 the pulling down of the strongholds is followed by the casting down of imaginations. Those imaginations are the garbage I described previously. Added to that is "every high thing that exalteth itself against the knowledge of God." This could be a catchall for anything you or I could imagine which is thrown in the face of God's knowledge. This could include every conceivable hindrance, impediment, opposition, tradition, or thought process.

Then the crowning blow—"bringing into captivity every thought to the obedience of Christ." (v. 5b) Now, I call upon you to imagine that happening to you. Every stronghold pulled down, every imagination cast down, every high thing put down, and every thought in your mind brought under the blessed captivity of Jesus! If that has just happened to you, do you expect that life for you will be any different than before? *What a foolish question! Of course it would be drastically changed!* you are thinking. And, of course, you are right. But that is not all. What about a world out there that needs straightening out? How about other unsettled accounts which are on my mind? How about the disobediences

of others out there? The answer comes ringing in 2
Corinthians 10:6, "And having in a readiness to revenge
all disobedience when your obedience is fulfilled." How
about that? When the strongholds are pulled down in
you and me, that is the starting point of a blessed chain-
reaction of liberation beginning with us! Can you imagine it? Fantastic!

Now that we have walked through the Scripture passage, let's go a little further. I have saved this for now
because I want you to remember precisely how to do it.
Here are the steps I use:

1. Be sure you're sure you're saved. Be sure you have
called upon the name of the Lord with the result that
something has happened in you to change you forever
(Rom. 10:13, "For whosoever shall call upon the name
of the Lord shall be saved").

2. Recognize that there is a war, that this war was
won by Jesus at Calvary, and that you must win the
battles moment by moment, day by day, week by week
on the battlefield of your mind.

3. Recognize that strongholds exist. Go back to the
tree of bondage and recognize which fruit are evident in
your life.

4. Realize that only God's power through Jesus
Christ can remove them. Capitalize on Philippians 4:13,
"I CAN DO ALL THINGS THROUGH CHRIST
WHICH STRENGTHENETH ME."

5. Identify the stronghold. Call it what it is. Take the
first name that comes to your mind as its true identity.
If it is gluttony, call it that. If it is lust, so identify it.

6. Confess the specific stronghold and acknowledge it as a sin in God's eyes. You see, sin both protects and perpetuates the stronghold and must be confessed.

7. Believe God for the tearing down of the strongholds, casting down of the imaginations, putting down of the high things, and the bringing of every thought in your mind captive to Jesus. Visualize those actions taking place, remembering the bulldozer, the chalkboard, the garbage, etc.

8. Ask Jesus to free you from these negative forces by His life in you (1 John 4:4*b*, "Greater is he that in you than he who is in the world").

9. Now thank Him and praise Him by faith for setting you free. Remember the words in 1 John 5:14-15, "This is the confidence that we have in Him; that if we ask anything according to his will, he heareth us; and if we know that he hear us, we know that we have the petitions that we desired of him."

10. Make restitution where needed. Ask God how to implement this process of restitution. Remember that, in general terms, the sin need be confessed no wider than the knowledge of it. Be sure then when your liberation begins and gains momentum you will want to pass it on, and restitution will be one of the expressions of this contagion.

A Prayer of Confession

I have used the following prayer (or one similar) all over the world with amazing blessings and results. Why don't you read it aloud right now?

I believe that Jesus Christ is the Son of God. He has come in the flesh, born of a virgin, and lived a sinless life. I confess that He died for me on Calvary, was buried, and three days later arose from the tomb, victorious over death, hell, and the grave. He proved himself alive by many infallible proofs, and He ascended into heaven.

He was crowned and seated at the right hand of God the Father. He sent His Holy Spirit into the world as He had promised. I do now acknowledge that I have trusted Him as my Savior and do now confess him to be both Savior and Lord. My body is the dwelling place of the Holy Spirit. The devil has no place in me and no power over me. I am a new creation "created in Christ Jesus unto good works." I am made righteous with the righteousness of Jesus. I have good standing before the throne of God because I am in Christ Jesus.

I now take a stand against every lie the devil has ever told me, and I refuse every lie he would now try to tell me. I take every piece of ground I have ever given him, break every contract I have ever made with him, and close every door I have ever opened to him, knowingly or unknowingly, intentionally or unintentionally. I come against every stronghold that he has constructed in my life.

Believing that the weapons in my hands are not carnal but mighty through God to the pulling down of strongholds, casting down imaginations with every high thing that exalts itself against the knowledge of God, I bring into captivity every thought unto the obedience of Christ.

I believe that the Bible gives me word of the will of God. I believe that this is the will of God for my life—even my freedom. I now claim my freedom and receive it in Jesus' Name. I DO NOW THANK AND PRAISE GOD FOR MY FREE-DOM. I CAN AND WILL THINK FREE. I CAN AND WILL PRAY FREE. I CAN AND WILL WITNESS FREE, BECAUSE I AM FREE. I can and do now choose Galatians 5:1 as being true of me. I will "stand fast in the liberty wherewith Christ has made me free, and will not be entangled with the yoke of bondage."

The knowledge of the truth is making us free and since the written Word is united with the Living Word, I am becoming free indeed (John 8:32,36).

Free to be me, God,
I really am free;
Free to become what You want me to be;
Free to decide whether I should be Lord,
Or be Your slave and obey Your Word.

Freedom, possession that makes me like You,
Frightens me, God, when the meaning seeps
   through!
Blessing or curse, Lord, condemned to be free?
Free, but responsible, free to be me!

Free to life fully, to follow Your way,
Give myself wholly to die every day;

Free to be real, God, to strip off my mask,
Be your creation, it's all that I ask.[1]

NOTE
1. WORDS, Kate Wilkins Wooley © Copyright 1970 • Broadman Press. All rights reserved.

10

A New Tree Grows in Barbara
(The Tree of Freedom
and Acceptance)

In chapters 7 and 8 we discussed the terrible Tree of Bondage. Let me remind you I am aware of the problem with illustrations. They tend to break down under too much weight. Any illustration is imperfect. My "tree" illustrations are no exceptions. I have accepted them from the Lord and have presented them to you with the expectation that they could be a blessing of illumination they have been to me.

Many seem to be receiving blessings wherever I share these truths. Remember I have been a first-grade teacher and tend to look at the world through such eyes. So receive these illustrations (in this chapter and others) for what they are, simple picture messages for the imparting of deeper spiritual truths.

I have sought to show you, via my particular spiritual journey from rejection, the nature of bondage and the beginning processes of liberation. For me the nature of that bondage was best described in the illustration of The Tree of Bondage. You may have different fruit on your tree than I had on mine, but I think you got the point. We have walked through in the previous chapter and talked of uprooting the tree, tearing down the strongholds, and bringing the soul into freedom.

In this chapter we will view a new tree, The Tree of Freedom and Acceptance. See page 135.

A part of the process in the destruction of strongholds is ultimately "clearing the land." Whatever illustration you have used in your personal approach to the matter of your liberation, the next important matter for consideration is *the production of proper fruit.* Whether you have seen the "bulldozer" of God's truth and the power of Jesus' Name and blood uproot strongholds or a chalkboard erased of "bad news," we next affirm the need of a good tree, a proper garden, a chalkboard filled with "good news."

I can't resist sharing with you something that has come to mind with this paragraph. It is very personal and very important in the process of my healing and liberation. If you have not already assumed by now, through what I have written, that I am a confronter, I will confirm it now. Jack is not a confronter.

I will go looking for a confrontation, and Jack will walk a mile around one. We had been married, at the time of this episode, twenty-five years, and we had maybe five major confrontations that I had not initiated. Trips to and from the airport were usually the occasions of our confrontations. That also had a special meaning to me because one day I found out why. Everytime Jack left on a plane my mind and emotions reminded me of Daddy leaving me when I was twelve years of age.

Back to my point. (Jack claims that if you ask me

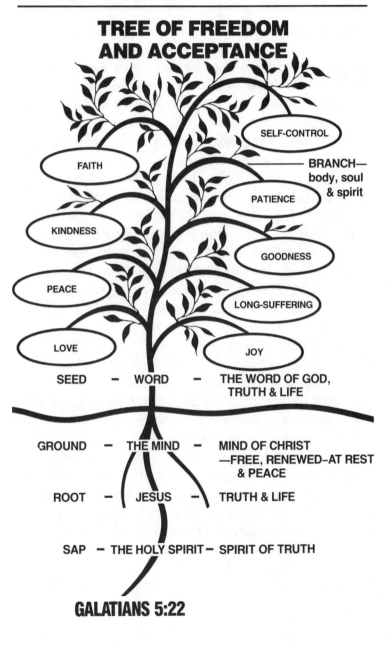

TREE OF FREEDOM AND ACCEPTANCE

SELF-CONTROL

FAITH

BRANCH— body, soul & spirit

PATIENCE

KINDNESS

GOODNESS

PEACE

LONG-SUFFERING

LOVE

JOY

SEED — WORD — THE WORD OF GOD, TRUTH & LIFE

GROUND — THE MIND — MIND OF CHRIST —FREE, RENEWED–AT REST & PEACE

ROOT — JESUS — TRUTH & LIFE

SAP — THE HOLY SPIRIT — SPIRIT OF TRUTH

GALATIANS 5:22

what time it is, I will tell you how to build a watch! Hang on—we'll get there!) This particular trip to the airport proved (to me) to be one of the most exciting and liberating experiences of our married life. But for Jack, it was not so. He was physically ill for two weeks afterwards.

This is what happened. As usual we had experienced a slight misunderstanding and were discussing it en route to the airport. (Well, I was discussing it anyway!) As I continued to yak-yak about whatever we were discussing, I noticed Jack becoming more and more tense. Well, we finally came to the airport, and I was seeing him off. I asked him, "Is there something wrong?" Well, he exploded. He sputtered and fumed and all but cussed as he unloaded twenty-five years of pent-up feelings. He told me what I knew he had been thinking for all those years and more.

I stood there as his "ultimate confrontation" washed over me like a fountain and allowed it to set me free from a bondage that Jack had ignorantly and unconsciously brought upon me. How can I explain it? I was pleading for this confrontation and had been for a quarter of a century. I had unconsciously been pushing for this confrontation all my life. Finally someone cared enough to confront me. I returned to the car. (This confrontation took place inside the airport terminal. Jack said that of all places for a confrontation to occur, the third-largest airport in the world took the cake!) When I arrived back at the car where our daughter, Tammy, was waiting, I related what had just happened. She answered simply and quietly, "Mother, why don't you plant a new garden?" I responded as quietly as her question, "I believe I will!"

At that precise moment I received from God the idea of the Tree of Bondage and The Tree of Freedom and Acceptance.

Now we will examine the Tree of Freedom and Acceptance much like we examined the Tree of Bondage, beginning at ground level. I want to remind you at this point of a wonderful passage of Scripture. In order to receive the impact of the special verse I need to show you the whole passage found in Isaiah 61:1-3. In this incomparable passage, which records the Messianic declaration of our Lord, we have a clear commitment on His part to our liberation. Read slowly the following words:

> The Spirit of the Lord God is upon me, because the Lord has anointed me to preach good tidings to the poor; he has sent me to heal the broken-hearted, to proclaim liberty to the captives, and the opening of the prison to those who are bound; to proclaim the acceptable year of the Lord. And the day of vengeance of our God; to comfort all who mourn, to console those who mourn in Zion, to give them beauty for ashes, the oil of joy for mourning, the garment of praise for the spirit of heaviness; THAT THEY BE CALLED THE TREES OF RIGHTEOUSNESS, THE PLANTING OF THE LORD, THAT HE MIGHT BE GLORIFIED (Capitalized emphases mine).

So you see, somewhat in line with my simple illustration, Jesus has come to liberate us so we might be *trees of righteousness.*

Now to the tree. Mark the page on which is found the illustration, and let's begin. We begin, as before, with a seed, which is the Word of God, the truth as revealed in the Scriptures and made real through the Holy Spirit. From the seed of truth grows the Tree of Freedom and Acceptance. Now move in your examination of the illustration to beneath the surface and the word "ground." It is, as we saw before, the mind. But the bright prospects here are found in the fact that we have the mind of Christ. We move further down to the root structure to find that Jesus, instead of self, is the tap root or main root. He is both Truth and Life. The life of Jesus, made real by His Spirit (the Holy Spirit) comprises the sap or life of the tree. It is the Spirit of Truth, coursing through the Tree of Freedom and Acceptance that brings about the production of the blessed fruit.

Now, of the fruit on our very special tree, we have a wonderful verse of Scripture in Galatians 5:22 (ASV).

> But the fruit of the Spirit is love, joy, peace, longsuffering, kindness, goodness, faithfulness, meekness [gentleness], self-control; against such there is no law.

This cluster of fruit is described after a lengthy list of the works of the flesh. So we have the *works* of the flesh contrasted to the *fruit* of the Spirit. Before we engage in this blessed "fruit inspection" let me make a couple of suggestions that might be helpful to you.

First, they are listed as fruit, not works. Fruit is

produced by natural process. Work requires effort. You never saw a tree straining and struggling to produce. Its fruit comes from the natural processes at work in its system from root to limb. It will be so in our spiritual fruit-bearing.

Second, the differing qualities are described as "fruit" (singular). This is probably more significant than one would normally suspect at first. The fruit is singular in the sense that it is one fruit with many expressions. The cluster is always together.

One cannot examine the list of the nine-fold fruit and find superficial comfort in being able to point to five or six or seven of these qualities in his or her life. When the Spirit of God produces in the life, these qualities are *always* there and are always together. The fruit of the Spirit both neutralizes and replaces the fruit we examined on the Tree of Bondage. It might be interesting for us to apply each quality of fruit on the good tree against the fruit on the terrible tree. I will make some applications as we go along. Let's go fruit inspecting!

Love

Love is the quality that pervades all God has done for us. Its nature is to be found in every one of the qualities to be mentioned in this chapter. In fact let us look ahead and preview the relationship of love to the other expressions of fruit.

Joy may be perceived as love *rejoicing*. Peace may be viewed as love *reposing*. Longsuffering can be taken as love *forbearing*. Kindness might be recognized as love *relating.* Goodness could be love *behaving.* Faithfulness finds love *believing.* Gentleness reveals love *caring.* Self-control shows love *mastering.*

What does love neutralize or negate on the Tree of Bondage? Love destroys *fear.* In fact we have already viewed 1 John 4:18 which says, "There is no fear in love; but perfect love casteth out fear, because fear hath torment. But he who fears hath not been made perfect in love."

For liberation to be initiated, effected, and maintained, love must take center stage. The kind of love we are discussing here has nothing to with the cheap, self-pleasing quality sung and talked about in show business. It is nothing short of the love of God planted in the human spirit by the Holy Spirit. It is a quality that unregenerate mankind knows nothing about. We must remember it does not come by *trying* but by trusting God and responding to His love. First John 4:19 says it clearly, "We love him because he first loved us." I might paraphrase that and say, "We *are able* to love because He first loved us." Thus it is with His love—that we love Him, and with that same love we are able to love others. We dare not leave this point until this realization dawns upon us: This and every quality we are going to examine are supernatural in origin and exercise. These are borne by the Holy Spirit. He is supernatural. We are here seeing supernatural production.

Next, love wipes out hate, murder, bitterness, resentment, and jealousy. These cannot cohabit with love.

The fact is that love has a destructive effect on all the fruit of the Tree of Bondage.

Peace

One of my favorite and most used passages is in Isaiah 26:3, "Thou wilt keep him in perfect peace whose mind is stayed on thee, because he trusteth in thee." One of Jesus' great promises is found in John 14:27, "My peace I leave with you, my peace give I unto you . . . Let not your heart be troubled, neither let it be afraid." He further said in John 16:33, "These things have I spoken unto you, that in me ye might have peace. In the world ye shall have tribulation; but be of good cheer, I have overcome the world." We are enjoined in 1 Thessalonians 5:13 to "be at peace among yourselves." In 1 Peter 3:11 we are exhorted to "seek peace and ensue [pursue] it." Paul reminds us in 2:14,15 that "He [Jesus] is our peace," and in being that we have become "one new man, making peace." "Peace!" ("Shalom!") was and still is a common greeting among the people of Israel.

As love replaces hate, peace replaces fear and anxiety. Love strikes a death-blow to defensiveness. Anger and depression cannot long live in an atmosphere of peace. What a wonderful combination of counsel and promise is found in Philippians 4:6-7! "Be careful [anxious] for nothing, but in everything by prayer and supplication, with thanksgiving, let your requests be made known to God. And the *peace of God* which passeth all understanding shall keep your hearts and minds through Christ Jesus" (Italics mine).

James reminds us that "the fruit of righteousness is sown in peace by those who make peace" (Jas. 3:18).

As you view the Tree of Freedom and Acceptance welcome the peace of God to your heart.

Kindness

I discovered it rather impossible continually to be kind while trying to cope in life. I could fake it for brief intervals but could blow it more often than not. I can identify with the little girl who was heard praying, "Lord, would you please make all the bad people good and all the good people nice?" One of the features of life on this planet, as it becomes more and more crowded, is irritation that expresses itself in unkindness. But as we are freed from the bondage and deception of rejection the Spirit of God produces genuine, caring kindness. I look forward, as I am sure you do, to both picking and sharing the fruit of kindness.

Faith (or Faithfulness)

I come closer and closer to *overwhelmed* as I view the list of the fruit of His tree! Praise the Lord that I don't have to struggle to have faith. It is a gift of God, "not of works, lest any man should boast" (Eph. 2:8*b*,9). Faithfulness is the capacity to remain true to a commitment. You and I have made so many resolutions, new beginnings, and false starts that desperation has set in for most of us. God's faithfulness in our behalf and in us gives us the capacity to be faithful in purpose and productivity.

All the fruit on the Tree of Bondage is hindering in its influence in our lives. Faithfulness neutralizes this hindering force.

Self-Control

What can be spoken of this worthy trait? It is really a picture of Jesus in control of the life. Have you seen someone whose calm approach to life instilled in you a deep desire to get a new grip on your life? I have, and I am determined to allow this fruit to develop and grow on my tree. Pray with me for a "bumper crop."

Patience (Longsuffering)

Oh boy, do I draw a blank in the flesh on this one! It's good that this is a fruit of the Spirit! I was absent the day they handed out patience. I really like the original word in the King James Version—"longsuffering." That suggests the ability to suffer in the long run. I'm not even good at "shortsuffering"! How thrilling to anticipate and experience patience in the new crop off of the Tree of Freedom and Acceptance.

Goodness

Have you noticed how down-to-earth and practical these descriptives are? The world needs this fruit as

desperately as it needs any. The absence of old-fash-
ioned goodness may be the severest hindrance to evan-
gelism as any in the church. A revival of goodness
among Christians would surely result in a sweeping
revival in the whole church.

Gentleness

Some folks have a kind of gentleness which comes
with their personality pattern. Others are about as gentle as a rhino bull in a china shop. Some of us who are
confronters tend to come under the latter category, I'm
afraid! But nothing is more amazing and awe-inspiring
as the "raging bull" who has been tranquilized by grace
and tamed with Spirit-borne tenderness. Jack and I
happen to know the man who was termed "the meanest
man in professional football" by many, John Bramlett.
The escapades of John are legend in the annals of pro
football. He was never satisfied with tackling someone.
He desired to be more exotic and break someone's finger
or nose or twist their ear almost off! And off the football
field he was worse! But one day this wild man met Jesus
Christ and was transformed into a teddy bear! In Jesus
he is as gentle as a lamb! Only in Christ can such a
change occur.

Joy

You will notice that I have listed the fruit in my own
order. I wanted to frame it in Love and Joy. I guess I
have put joy last because it reminds me of the well-
known acrostic: Jesus first; others second; and you last,

making up the word JOY. Jack declares that the only folks in the world who can afford to be incorrigibly joyful are Christians. Anyone else who is always doing so just doesn't understand the situation!

Joy seems to deserve in my mind a crowning position because I am finding that the more I allow the Holy Spirit to produce His blessed fruit in me, the more I am liberated to rejoice in myself, as well as in right relationships with others. "Joy unspeakable and full of glory."

Have you heard me saying this is my tree? Have I claimed here that my tree is bearing this fruit, all of it, all the time? I wish it were true. Sometimes the crop is spotty and sparse, but the crop is getting better, the potential is thrilling, and the prospects are encouraging. As I was working on this chapter, Jack reminded me of a book title he ran across. Jack majors on catchy titles and was really "caught" by this one. In fact, he wishes he had thought of it. The title is *Tomorrow I Will Be Perfect*. It was written by a baseball player, struggling with imperfection, but anticipating better days. I'm going to remember that title and remind myself of its truth as it has to do with me, my present, and my future. And you should too! One tomorrow, not long from now at worst, you and I will awake in His presence. The Bible expresses it infinitely better than I could, "Beloved, now we are the sons of God, and it doth not yet appear what we shall be, but we know that when he shall appear, WE SHALL BE LIKE HIM for we shall see him as he is" (1 John 3:2, caps mine). You ask, "How can you be so sure?" I answer you like a young boy did when asked how he knew that he was saved. "I don't know how I know; I just know I know!" I don't understand it; I cannot fathom it; I have some trouble envisioning it; but, praise the Lord, I KNOW IT!

A New Tree is growing in Barbara, The Tree of Freedom and Acceptance. At times I smell a faint odor from some of the putrid fruit of the old tree (and sometimes a shocking whiff), but a new crop is under production.

Has it dawned on you, as we have walked among this blessed display of fruit, that what we are really talking about is nothing less than the character of Christ Himself? Yes, these are the character qualities of our Savior. They can be produced in you and me because He who possesses them is alive in us, prepared to exercise His eternal wisdom and employ his eternal power in and through us for victory. Victory is not a prize I win by achievement. It is a Person I receive by faith. First John 5:4 says, ". . . and this is the victory that overcometh the world, even our faith." We have the *victory* because we have received the *Victor* into our hearts—the Lord Jesus Christ.

We have been reminded in John 15 of the essence of our relationship with God. Jesus has taught, "I am the vine, and my father is the husbandman [vinedresser]. Ye are the branches. He that abideth in me and I in him, bringeth forth much fruit. Herein is my Father glorified, that ye bear much fruit. Then shall ye be called my disciples" (vv. 1,5,8).

As we allow the tree to grow in us, and the fruit to be borne, we will come to a sense of who we are in Christ. I will be dealing with this in the next chapter.

11
Discovering Our True Identity

While I am writing this volume Jack is in the process of writing one we believe will serve as a companion volume to this one. In this chapter and the next there will be some overlapping with his work which is entitled *God's New Creation.* His thesis will center in the believer's essential identity as it is based on the covenant relationship with God through Jesus Christ. This overlapping, we have discovered, is both intentional and inevitable. We have agreed that this work would not be complete without some basic understanding of who we are in Christ. This we believe to be necessary both to the initiation of our freedom and the preservation of it through implementation.

Jack and I have worked through this material together and are living through the adventure of continued and deepening liberation. We believe that our liberation from all that keeps us from being like Jesus is the essential element in and the basic purpose of salvation. It is more than an event. It is a process. Ultimately it is a consummation. I have sought to be careful to avoid speaking of my liberation in the past tense, though there was a point in time when it began to happen.

I have spoken of it again and again in a continuing sense, and that is precisely what it is. To see what I am talking about in three tenses will help the reader immensely. I look upon my liberation in these three tenses. It has happened at a point of departure. I am moving toward a destination with confident expectations that one day I will be like Jesus because I will see Him as He is! But between the departure point and the desired destination I am under construction, in process, a becomer. Within this context this book is being written.

You will find Jack's writing vastly different from mine. And for good reasons! We are different in our thinking patterns, in our emotional patterns, in our behavior patterns. In fact we are drastically different! So you would expect that in our presentations there would be a different method, different order, and different slants of communication. I have been and will be sharing with you as it happened in my life.

If you feel you are riding on a roller-coaster, welcome to the party! That is exactly how it has been. If you feel you are being drowned in illustrations and choked with words, take some time off. Ponder what you have read. Shelve what doesn't seem to scratch where you are itching. Not everything on these pages is for everybody. You will be able to identify with me at some points and in others will be left with that high-and-dry feeling. Not to worry. If you feel like it is getting too complicated, let up and take a few minutes or a few hours off. You didn't get where you are in a day, and it isn't likely you get where you desire in a day. A part of all our bondages is that feature which belongs to time and space. God views us from a vantage point entirely free from the time-space bondage. If we truly have the mind of Christ, as we are told in 1 Corinthians 2:15, we can surely anticipate that a "Jesus mentality" will begin to free us from this prison of time and space.

Be that as it may, we turn now to the blessed discovery of our identities as individuals and how we fit into the Body of Christ. Jack and I believe that one of the deep-down problems in modern-day Christianity is one of *identity.* We could not be expected to act as we ought until we discover who we are. Jack speaks of a law in human behavior which states that we all tend to act like what or who we believe ourselves to be. That is not only the means with which we relate to ourselves but to others as well. So without a sense of who we are, our essential identity, we are without a meaningful relationship with either ourselves or one another. We will have neither of these until we have a working idea of what God views us to be, what He spoke in His Word about who we are, and how He expects us to view ourselves. This chapter has to do with your identity and mine as seen through the eyes of Scripture from God's vantage point.

Our model for this chapter is found in the illustration entitled Finding Out Who We Are in Christ. See page 150.

Who We Were

We can best begin to understand who we are by viewing the dark background of our past before Christ.

FINDING OUT WHO WE ARE IN CHRIST

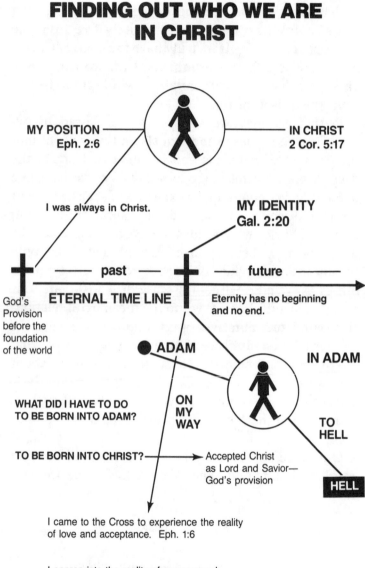

MY POSITION — IN CHRIST
Eph. 2:6   2 Cor. 5:17

I was always in Christ.

MY IDENTITY
Gal. 2:20

—— past ——   —— future ——

ETERNAL TIME LINE

God's
Provision
before the
foundation
of the world

Eternity has no beginning
and no end.

ADAM   IN ADAM

WHAT DID I HAVE TO DO
TO BE BORN INTO ADAM?

ON
MY
WAY

TO
HELL

TO BE BORN INTO CHRIST? ——→ Accepted Christ
as Lord and Savior—
God's provision

HELL

I came to the Cross to experience the reality
of love and acceptance. Eph. 1:6

I appropriate the reality of my personal
experience by obeying Luke 9:23 moment
by moment.

Our past goes all the way back to Adam. That must be both acknowledged and somewhat understood in order to grasp who we are. Our past identity is tied to Adam. We were, in fact, in Adam when he chose to sin. Can you understand that? I know it's hard but please try.

Let me see if I can help. If Adam had died before he had children, you and I would not have existed. We were potential in him the very day he sinned. He was, in a sense, the representative of all of us yet unborn. When he sinned, we sinned. Doesn't seem fair, does it? Stick with me, though, because it comes out wonderfully. So, as unjust as it might appear, we were represented long before we were born. Our representative, Adam, failed to represent us properly and chose to sin—and in doing so affected the whole human race.

So you and I were born with a bent with which we had nothing to do. That bent was toward sin. It was such a serious inclination that we have invented a big theological word for it called "depravity." It simply means, I am told, that we are touched and tainted with sin in every part of us and totally helpless in ourselves to do anything to remedy it. The description of us is not hidden from us. The Bible is forthright when it comes to speaking of our condition outside of Christ. In a brief word it is described like this, "As in Adam all die, even so in Christ shall all be made alive" (1 Cor. 15:22).

To be blunt about it you and I were *born dead!* We were a problem to begin with. As if that were not serious enough, listen to the really bad news! I will merely list what the Bible says about who we were:

We were dead in trespasses and sins.

We walked according to the course of this world.

We walked according to the devil, the prince of the power of the air.

We were indwelt with the spirit of disobedience, old slew-foot himself.

We conducted life in the lusts of the flesh, fulfilling our own selfish desires.

We were by nature the children of wrath.

We were strangers and foreigners from God.

We were aliens from the commonwealth of Israel.

We were strangers to the covenants of promise.

We were without hope and without God in the world.

Now all the above is found in Ephesians 2:1-3 and verses 12 and 19. Pretty grim picture, isn't it? Grim, yes, but accurate! In your illustration for this chapter you will first find yourself, as you were, in the circle just to the lower right of the middle—IN ADAM! You and I were in Adam when he sinned; we were born in Adam. We had to do absolutely nothing to get there. We remained there until Jesus came along and liberated us from our prison IN ADAM. Had we stayed in Adam our final destination would have been hell. And we would have received exactly what we deserved! So nearly in the words of a famous news commentator, "And that's the way we were!"

What We Are

Back to our illustration! At the top of the illustration

we see the circle with a figure in it described by the words on either side, MY POSITION and IN CHRIST. The Scriptures representing our identity are as immediately encouraging as the other Scriptures were discouraging. We are told in Ephesians 2:6, "And hath raised us up together, and made us sit together in heavenly places IN CHRIST JESUS" (caps mine). In 2 Corinthians 5:17 we are further informed, "Therefore if any man be in Christ, he is a new creature [creation]; old things are passed away; behold, all things are become new."

I want to share with you a feature that most Christians have never thought of, much less understood. On the illustration please notice the line moving downward to the left from the circle IN CHRIST to the cross at left center. On the line you will read these words, "I was always in Christ." Don't try to understand this, but merely listen and let it into your spirit. Your mind won't do much about it at first, except possibly show a "tilt" or "not-found" sign! Historically there was a time when you and I were in Adam. But when we were placed into Christ we were posited into His past and future, as well as His present! Once we were there, as God views it, we had always been there. Historically and legally the only past now of record that we have is—you guessed it—IN CHRIST! In summary it can be said, "I was in Adam, dead, condemned, lost, separated, without hope, and without God. Adam was my past, present, and my future. But I came to Christ, repented, and believed, and He came into me. Now I am IN HIM. Now that I am IN HIM I am in His past, present, and future. That is the only past I have! Nothing is left as evidence for the devil to accuse!" Isn't that something? Do you understand it? Don't try! Just praise the Lord that, like many other facets of our faith, it doesn't have to be understood to be enjoyed!

What Happened to You

You and I were in Adam. We are now in Christ. How did it happen? Through God's prearranged plan, salvation existed before the need of it, "before the foundation of the world." So as you view the illustration you see the cross at middle left at the beginning of the line across the center of the page, the eternal lifeline. At the middle of the line you observe another cross marking the time and place you and I were brought individually into Christ. At that moment in each of us, what Paul reports in Galatians 2:20, occurred in us, "I am crucified with Christ; nevertheless I live; yet not I, but Christ liveth in me, and the life I now live in the flesh, I live by the faith of the Son of God who loved me and gave himself for me." My identity was achieved at the cross. I don't need to expend any effort to be crucified. That has already happened. But, having been crucified, I now live a new life IN HIM. (I have moved from the plural to the singular for personal emphasis!)

So now I have a new ID, a new identity! I am not what or who I used to be! I am now in a new realm—IN CHRIST. I came to the cross to experience this reality of love and acceptance. I am acceptable because I have been made aceptable by His work on the cross. I have been placed into Christ in time past; it is a present reality; and I will evermore be in Christ. That is my new environment, my new condition, my new position, and my new identity. Moment by moment, hour by hour, day by day, week by week, and month after month, into the years, I am identified with Christ and have the privilege of living according to that identity.

Please take the time to observe the illustration on Finding Who We Are in Christ. Reread the sections of this chapter that are not quite clear and relate them to the illustration where needed. The picture, in this case, may be worth *more* than a thousand words.

Take a moment to celebrate your identity as a believer, even though this information may be new and strange to your ears. Celebrate it by verbalizing it over and over again. Say something like, "I am new . . . a new creation. I am in Christ . . . in His past, present, and future. In Christ old things have passed away; all things have become new. I don't understand it, but, PRAISE THE LORD, I believe it." That will do for a start, but be careful. It might be habit forming!

It is really all right for you to enjoy being you. The new you is worth loving, and loving yourself is absolutely essential to overcoming rejection, breaking all connected bondage, and living a liberated life. Don't leave these pages without realizing that you have both a right and a responsibility to believe and declare to be true everything God has said in His Word about you. That is THE GOOD NEWS. What do we do now that we have been thusly informed? Come to the next chapter and let's talk about *appropriation.*

12
Appropriating Our Identity

It is one thing to know something. It is quite another to believe it to the degree that we benefit from it. This chapter is written so you might not be content with simply knowing—but go on to appropriate your identity.

I wish you were with me right now. I would be all too glad to show you my favorite "toy." It would surely prepare you to appropriate your true identity. I have in view my "toy." It is a hand-sewn cloth caterpillar about eight inches long, three inches high, and six inches around. You know right away, the first time you see it, what it is. It has five little legs on either side, multicolored eyes which bulge out, and a little yellow bulb for a nose. He's a right *wormy* little fellow! (or "she" in our case, girls!)

I may assume if "it" (as I will refer to "it" from here on) were alive it would act as wormy as it looks, thinking wormy thoughts and engaging in wormy ways. But then that's all you can expect from a worm. Worms do wormy things—they think wormy, crawl wormy, and live wormy. (English students might think it should be "wormily" . . . adverb modifying a verb! Have it your way!) Everything is consistent. Worm is as worm does and worm does as worm is. As long as it "is" it "does." What's inside comes out. What's in the well comes up in the bucket. What comes around goes around.

If my worm were to bear any offspring they would all naturally be worms, each a chip off the old worm! And generation after generation worm life would be passed on. That's the way it was with you and me. We were IN ADAM, quite another species than God intended for man to be—a worm, if you please. I have always wondered why the folks who revised the first verse of "At the Cross" changed the words, "For such a worm as I . . ." Were they trying to make us look better than we are? "Sinners" are like that worm, stuck with a worm nature, filled with filth, and imprisoned in a terrible behavior pattern. Without hope, condemned to "worminess" here and hereafter in time and eternity! That is unless something miraculous happens. Leave this thought process. Then go with me—back to "worm."

My worm is no ordinary worm. I pick it up and find a zipper on its belly side that runs the length of its little body. I grab the zipper handle located right under its nose and unzip it. A strange and mysterious thing begins to happen. As I fold down the sides of the caterpillar, another body appears, that of a butterfly! And the wings! How can I describe them? They stretch about sixteen inches from tip to tip. The zipper is now on the underside of the *butterfly*. Just as I unzipped it I now zip it up and have done with "worm" forever (or until I use this illustration again). Worm is no longer worm.

Worm is butterfly! Worm has become a new creation, a butterfly. Now it has a new identity, a new nature, and new capacities. It has butterfly thoughts and butterfly ways. It flies instead of crawling. It soars instead of inching along at ground level. It rests in trees, not under clods. It floats above the earthfolks instead of being "squashed" beneath their feet. I like my toy best in the latter shape. I need to look at the worm every now and then to remind me of what I was IN ADAM. I don't need to think about the worm for long, however. I need to think "butterfly" constantly. It represents what I have become, a new creation with a new nature, new thought patterns, and new abilities to behave differently.

I use my "toy" to illustrate the miraculous change that has occurred and is occurring in my life. Wherever I share the truths about rejection and acceptance I employ my worm. Everyone readily identifies. It is the best illustration I can conceive of to picture the work of Christ in our lives. Face it. Only to another caterpillar is a caterpillar beautiful and desirable, unless maybe to a small boy who loves woolly worms, garter snakes, daddy long legs, and other assorted critters. Every biology student knows that a certain kind of caterpillar goes through a stage known as "metamorphosis" which is a large word meaning "a big change." As you know, instincts built within that little worm by the Creator cause it to go somewhere by itself, spin up in a cocoon, and lie there as it were in suspended animation, waiting for that "great day." He goes from one life toward another and emerges as a butterfly, gorgeous and ready to fly. The slimy, wormy creature is transformed into a new creature, a butterfly, one of God's loveliest and most sought-after creatures.

Without Christ we were caterpillars, ikky, ugly, and slinky. Then we encounter the cross. We die to self. We experience metamorphosis. We move from one life form to another. Worm as worm meets cross and Christ. Worm becomes butterfly. Butterfly flies! No surprise! It is inherent in its new nature. And so with us. We emerge as something beautiful and radiant in the sight of God. We become "new creations" in Christ Jesus (2 Cor. 5:17).

Now, we are what we are because we have been made so by an act of God. There is no effort needed to be what we are as new creations. To stretch the illustration of the worm and butterfly we might facetiously imagine that the butterfly emerges, but without the knowledge that a metamorphosis has taken place. Its mind is not renewed to correspond to its new nature as a butterfly. It has the mind of a butterfly but has a "hangover mentality" from wormhood. This corresponds to a believer who tends toward carnal-mindedness. A new creation thinking and acting like an old one! Can you imagine it? A butterfly thinking and acting like a worm. It just doesn't fit! In order to act like a worm, the butterfly has to come down off its lofty perch or out of the wide, blue sky and slither on the grass or sidewalk. After a while it looks toward the sky, and something within it longs to soar, yet anticipations are frustrated by ignorance, and it is confined to the ground! Made to fly but in bondage to the past!

SCRIPTURES TO APPROPRIATE AND CONFESS DAILY

2 COR. 5:17 . . . . WHO YOU ARE
A NEW CREATION!

EPH. 1:6 . . . . ACCEPTED
IN THE BELOVED

EPH. 2:6 . . . . YOUR POSITION
IN CHRIST

GAL. 2:20 . . . . YOUR IDENTITY
IN CHRIST

ROM. 6:11 . . . . YOUR CHOICE...
YOUR WILL

LUKE 9:23 . . . . YOUR APPROPRIATION
& RESPONSIBILITY

GAL. 5:1 . . . . ACCEPTING
YOUR FREEDOM IN CHRIST

What I am talking about is truth and freedom unappropriated. What I want to talk with you about now is the matter of appropriation. I refer you to the illustration entitled Scriptures to Appropriate and Confess Daily found on page 161. I will simply give the Scripture and make some suggestions for practical exercises in your life.

2 Corinthians 5:17—Who You Are . . .
A New Creation

> Therefore, if any man be in Christ, he is a new creature: old things are passed away, behold, all things are become new.

Over and over again we have declared that what God says about us is true. This is the truth about us. We are no longer the "old man," the old has gone; the new has come. The way I made this a daily reality in my life was by memorizing this passage, putting it on cards, message pads, and the like, in order to remind myself of this great truth. I put these reminders on my mirror, in my purse, in different places in my Bible, and about my house. I also personalized the passage as I do others by saying, "Since Barbara is in Christ, she is a new creation; old things have passed away, behold, all things have become new in Barbara." When the devil or my mind brings up any thought contrary to this truth, I try to bring that thought captive to Jesus and write this passage on the chalkboard of my mind or visualize it written across the sky. Because my thoughts become my emotions and my emotions become my behavior, I must bring my thoughts into obedience to the Word of God.

Ephesians 1:6—"Accepted in the Beloved"

To the praise of the glory of his grace, wherein he hath made us accepted in the beloved.

Because God knows what He had made me, He can and does accept me in Christ. In the process of my self-talk (speaking to myself the truth) I can further say, BARBARA, YOU WILL NEVER BE REJECTED AGAIN. YOU ARE ACCEPTED IN THE BELOVED (JESUS CHRIST). I am accepted, not rejected, because when Jesus died for my sins in order to take them away, He also died for my rejection, and has taken it away.

What a terrific thought that Jesus "was made sin" for my sin in order to take it away; was rejected with my rejection that he might remove it; was made sick with my sicknesses in order to heal me; and bore my offenses that I might have no offense. "He was despised and rejected of men; a man of sorrows, and acquainted with grief . . . Surely he hath borne our griefs, and carried our sorrows" (Isa. 53:3,4).

Ephesians 2:6—Your Position in Christ

And hath raised us up together, and made us sit together in heavenly places in Christ Jesus"

My new identity and my new status of acceptance

bring me to a new position, a new location, in Christ.
I say, "God has raised Barbara up and has given her the
position in heavenly places in Christ." In some cases I
try to remember an illustration of a special moment of
pleasure with which to associate a Bible truth. When
Jack and I were parasailing in the Cayman Islands, I
remember being seated in the parachute harness being
lifted a hundred feet or so above the bay, looking down
on the beach. "Keep looking up!" may be a good suggestion regarding the second coming of Jesus, but I prefer
"Keep looking down!" as my motto regarding my lofty
position in Christ. Back to the parasailing illustration.
I remember being strapped in the harness and giving the
nod to the driver of the boat. As I said "yes" with a nod,
the boat operator revved the engine and took off. I was
lifted by the momentum of the boat and the drag of the
parachute into the atmosphere! What a moment of ex-
hilaration followed! But it was too soon ended. The lofty
position I have in Christ is permanent! Praise the Lord!
And God is waiting for your "yes!" I am reminded of
the time God spoke to young Samuel, and his answer
was, "Yes, Lord!" We have a stirring theme song at our
church that helps me in daily appropriation.

> I'll say "Yes, Lord, yes"
> To Your will and to Your way
> I'll say "Yes, Lord, yes"
> I Will trust You and obey.
> When Your Spirit speaks to me,
> With my whole heart I'll agree
> And my answer will be "Yes, Lord, yes."

Galatians 2:20—Your Identity in Christ

I am crucified with Christ: nevertheless I live; yet not I, but Christ liveth in me: and the life which I now live in the flesh I live by the faith of the Son of God, who loved me and gave himself for me.

I remind myself with this Scripture, "Barbara, you have been crucified with Christ (like Paul) and yet you live; yet it is not you that is living, Barbara, but Christ that is living in you; so the life you are now living is really lived from His resources."

At times when we are talking about this subject it seems more appropriate to use "identified" than "identity." Let me show you why. My identity lies in the fact that I, Barbara, was crucified with Him; I, Barbara, was buried with Him; I, Barbara, rose with Him; I, Barbara, ascended with Him; I, Barbara, am seated in the heavenlies with Him; and I, Barbara, am alive with Him now in this life. Thus I am IDENTIFIED with him in everything He has done in my behalf in order for me to perceive my IDENTITY.

When I entered the baptismal waters I thought that baptism was the perfect picture of Christ's death, burial, and resurrection. I know now that, in a more real way, it was a picture of Barbara's death, burial, and resurrection. In baptism I was visualizing my IDENTIFICATION with His death, burial, and resurrection because He had already made them real in me as a new IDENTITY.

I find it helpful to rehearse the following now and then:

> I AM BARBARA,
>   DAUGHTER OF ALICE AND BRYAN,
>   SISTER OF BILL,
>   WIFE OF JACK,
>   MOTHER OF TAM AND TIM,
>   GRANDMOTHER OF KIMBER,
>   TIMOTHY BRYAN, AND BLAKE,
>   FORMER SCHOOL TEACHER,
>   AUTHOR AND SPEAKER;
> BUT NONE OF THESE, AS MEANINGFUL AS THEY ARE, BRING THE JOY THAT COMPARES WITH MY BEING ABLE TO SAY,
> BARBARA, DAUGHTER OF THE KING, A PRINCESS, INDWELT WITH THE LIFE OF CHRIST . . . ACCEPTED IN HIM. (This is my good self-image.)

Romans 6:11—Your Choice . . . Your Will

> Likewise reckon ye also yourselves to be dead indeed unto sin, but alive unto God through Jesus Christ our Lord.

I have said it before; I'll say it again; and I say it now, "For the truth to keep on working in your life and mine we must keep making choices in correspondence to God's Word and will moment by moment, hour by hour, and day by day!" A daily ritual will prove helpful.

(At times it must be done many times a day!) When something happens that would formerly have set my strongholds on edge and caused an explosion within and without, I must simply reassert, "I, Barbara, having experienced Calvary in Christ, do now declare it so that I have died indeed unto sin and am alive only to God through Jesus!"

When I was doing this from performance-based acceptance I thought I was reckoning IN ORDER that I might be dead and then alive. Not so, as I realize now, but I reckon myself dead to sin and alive to God BECAUSE I AM dead to sin and alive to God. I am just confessing something that is already a reality in order to allow God to make it a reality in the manifestations of my life.

LUKE 9:23—Your Appropriation and Responsibility

And he said to them all, If any man will come after me, let him deny himself, and take up his cross daily, and follow me.

The prime word in that passage should be recognized as DAILY. There it is again! I am daily to bring my Calvary experience up to date in order that I might continuously be filled with the Spirit. That is my responsibility day by day on a continuous basis. My identity is a gift of God to me, but I must take the responsibility for appropriating it.

Galatians 5:1—Accepting Your Freedom in Christ

> Stand fast, therefore, in the liberty wherewith
> Christ hath made us free, and be not entangled
> again with the yoke of bondage.

Again, I personalize this by constantly saying, "Since
I have received liberty from my bondage, through
Christ I WILL NOT, I WILL NOT, I WILL NOT be
entangled again with the yoke of bondage."

Standing firm and staying free is merely a matter of
the will's cooperating with the truth and the power of
God. It is not the power of the will but the power that
comes from God when the will is exercised in accord-
ance with truth.

A Final Word

There is nothing left for me to say at this point. You
are a new creation in Christ. You are "accepted in the
beloved." Your position is "seated with Him in the
heavenly places in Christ Jesus." You are crucified with
Him. Your old life without Christ was nailed to the
cross. Your new identity allows Christ to live His life
through you. Your choice and your will are involved in
accepting and believing in the fact that you are now
dead to the self-life. This is not an exercise in mere
semantics. It works when we are willing to affirm all
Christ has done on our behalf. Your appropriation and
responsibility are bound up in your taking up your cross

daily, being identified with the cross-life, and denying yourself.

Finally, you need to accept your freedom in Christ. Talk about liberation, about the liberated woman, the liberated man! In Christ you are free indeed. "If therefore the Son shall make you free, ye shall be free indeed" (John 8:36). "If ye abide in my word, then you are true disciples of mine; and you shall know the truth, and the truth shall make you free" (John 8:31-32).

For a closing exercise to this chapter simply go back over the previous two paragraphs and personalize every word of my exhortation to you. Do it now!

13
Renewing the Mind

This may be the most important chapter in this book as far as the ongoing processes of liberation are concerned. I am not a psychologist, a counselor, or a preacher, but I am the custodian of a continuing experience I am pledged to share with whomever may benefit from it. So, as usual, let me present my testimony with this area of truth.

In the not-too-distant past my life was literally coming unraveled. I was a physical wreck, first of all. I had difficulty sleeping and was tired most of the time. I was a borderline anemic. I was overweight and couldn't seem to do anything to remedy it. I had frequent kidney problems. I had an unquenchable thirst. My eyesight was becoming affected. I had what is commonly known as "sinking spells." My hormones were out of balance. I began to consider what kind of operation I might need, since I had already undergone three surgeries removing certain of my "inner parts." I was hoping that most of what I was going through physically could be explained by the period of a woman's life known as menopause.

In addition to this, I was an emotional basket case.

I was depressed much of the time. When I was not depressed I was hyper. I was either hostile or deeply depressed in deepening and heightening cycles. I suspicioned that not one person in the world either understood me or loved me. In fact, there was a suspicion that the whole world was against me. I was filled with fear and anxiety. I frequently harbored thoughts of suicide. I was a problem to myself and others. I was no fun to be around. I was not dealing effectively with the past, the present, or the prospective future.

Spiritually, I was a picture of perfect confusion. I could not see anything that Jack taught, preached, or wrote working like he contended it would. I was very poor publicity for his books. In fact, on one occasion I said, "For all practical purposes we might as well call all your books in, as far as I am concerned. It is simply not working in my life!" I even doubted God's love for me. I was not sure about my place in the Body of Christ. My fellowship with God and man was vague and uncertain. However, I had not lost my immovable confidence in the Bible, the Word of God. (That is a pivotal feature in this whole story. And the simple truth here is: had it not been for the Word of God and my absolute faith in its reliability I would not be alive today—or, if alive, worse off than dead!)

All of this—my physical condition, my emotional posture, and my spiritual status—exerted unbelievable stress on every area of my life. Each area seemed to affect the other in further complicating situations. Mixed with these complications, shake in one other ingredient—I was traveling all over the North American continent with Jack and making several trips abroad. After one of these trips abroad my stress reached a peak. My stress further drove me to serious overeating, kept me from resting at night, and disrupted my thought processes. I would have been glad to have "a nervous breakdown" if someone had been kind enough to tell me how to have one! I probably would have had one problem which would have disallowed it. I couldn't find room in my already-filled schedule!

Everything was of major consequence in my mind. During the hostage crisis with Iran we had planned one of our trips abroad. I had become so involved with the families of the hostages that I was thinking about them more and more. Ted Koppel and I spent most late evenings together. (As if I didn't have enough problems already!)

On one trip abroad my crisis intersected Jack's. I thought he was going through the mid-life crisis. He insisted that he wasn't. (I am told denial is one of the signs!) The trip was a torrent of torments. If you have not found out by now: the menopause meeting the mid-life crisis is like the irresistible force meeting the immovable object. The crash occurred while we were on that trip abroad. It is an absolute wonder we made it home together or even in one piece. At one point Jack was ready to send me home alone, but, of course, never would have. I suspicioned the motives of some people in our group and their attitudes toward me and my husband. The fear I had harbored for years, that I would lose my reasoning powers like my mother did and go haywire, came back again with tornadic ferocity.

Do you know what I mean? Three bricks shy of a load! Bubble seriously off of middle. Elevator not going all the way to the top. Lights on, nobody home! Dipstick showing three quarts low! I wish I could have laughed then, but it wasn't all that funny.

My family laughs at me mixing metaphors and hyperboles. I remind myself of the fellow who said, "Don't get out on a limb, or they will pull the rug out from under you!" or, "Never look a gift horse in the middle of the stream!" I was acting much like a couple we had become acquainted with in California, "Boy, they are as weird as a two-dollar duck!" Just the other day I told Jack that something was "as plain as your hand on your face!" Well, I was acting as weird as that "two-dollar duck," and it was "as plain as my hand on my face!"

Back to the trip abroad. We did make it home. The pressure of the responsibilities of being the hostess had nearly done me in. We were happy to be home. In fact, we were overjoyed to be anywhere after that trip. One morning, a few days later, I woke up shaking, crying uncontrollably, and was virtually blind. It frightened me so much I tried to awaken Jack. Even then I couldn't tell him what was wrong. Jack had remembered that a friend on the trip, after noticing my extreme behavior, had offered a suggestion that I needed to see a nutritionist. Jack then called this friend, and she gave him the name of a nutritionist. She was called and my condition described. She immediately made some suggestions that gave some relief.

This was the first step in our determination to look

in every possible direction for my cure. We found that I was a borderline diabetic and had multiple allergies. Later it was confirmed I was a brittle diabetic which gave me a clues about why I had such an imbalance in my spiritual life—extremely high highs and terribly low lows. We looked in all directions at the same time for possible help, physical, emotional, and spiritual. Was it simply body chemistry? Or was it all emotional and mental? Or was it a case of demonic traffic? The answer we found to be *yes* and *no*. It involved all three and was isolated in none of the three.

The story has become longer than I intended, but I have shared it for at least two reasons. I wanted you to see how bad off I was, and I wanted you to be able to identify with my condition.

To make a longer story shorter, I was advised by both nutritionist and doctors that I must have a rigid physical regimen of eating, exercising, and resting. I sought to comply.

But somehow I knew deep down within me that, if this were going to work, I must have a mental overhaul, a re-word processing of my thought life, a complete renewing of the mind. In fact this project, of getting my mind together, had to have top priority, or none of the other would work. I was told I had to stay home for a year. Now, read this next sentence carefully. What I am about to relate became the means of so freeing me up that I was able to be up and with Jack in six weeks, and as Willie Nelson sings, "On the Road Again"!

Along with prescriptions, instructions, diets, and ex-

ercises I took a massive dose of Scripture, beginning
with Romans 12:1-2:

> I beseech you therefore, brethren, by the mercies
> of God, that ye present your bodies a living sac-
> rifice, holy, acceptable unto God, which is your
> reasonable service. And be not conformed to this
> world but be ye transformed by the renewing of
> your mind, that ye may prove what is that good,
> and acceptable, and perfect will of God.

I saw that this passage covered all three areas, the
body and the mind, as well as the spirit. So what tool
would I use to renew my mind? The Bible, of course! It
would form the curriculum of my thought life and be
the key to my eating, resting, and exercise! The Lord
then showed me Philippians 4:8-9: "Finally, brethren,
whatsoever things are true, whatsoever things are honest, whatsoever things are just, whatsoever things are
pure, whatsoever things are lovely, whatsoever things
are of good report; if there be any virtue, and if there
be any praise, think on these things." I saw the map my
mind must travel through the gates of TRUTH,
HONESTY, JUSTICE, PURITY, LOVELINESS,
GOOD REPORT, VIRTUE, AND PRAISE.

So I began my spiritual exercise program along with,
but in priority over, the physical matters. I determined
to set my mind on the Lord. I had memorized Isaiah
26:3: "Thou wilt keep him in perfect peace, whose mind
is stayed on thee: because he trusteth in thee."

I began to exercise early every morning, running
around the small lake at the center of our townhouse

complex. As I ran I confined my thought processes to these Scriptures that I am sharing with you. I memorized them from cards that I held in my hand as I ran. My mind needed to be reprocessed with His thoughts, not mine.

Shortly after I started this regimen I began to know Christ in a manner I never thought possible for me. Philippians 3:10 was becoming a reality in my life: "That I may know him, and the power of his resurrection, and the fellowship of his sufferings, being made conformable to his death."

About that time I was invited to bring the closing address at a large conference for women in Springfield, Missouri. Me? Why me? There were luminaries of national stature on the program, but I was to present the climactic closing message to the conference. My assigned topic was (Can you believe it?) "Think on These Things"! This was the theme of the conference. My assigned task was to tie all the discussions of the conference together and give the invitation to close the meeting.

No wonder God had directed me to those Philippian passages and that for months I had allowed them to permeate and saturate my entire being. God was preparing me for that very speaking engagement. I could hardly wait to get there! I carried one little sheet of paper with a simple outline on it. I prayed, "Lord, I know You are going to fleshen out this outline and make it live. I can't wait to stand up there and see and hear what You are going to do and say to us through me." Frankly, I wouldn't necessarily recommend being that brazen and confident all the time. Sometimes the Lord might not fleshen out the outline! But you see, He had spent weeks preparing me to deliver that message.

It was unbelievable. God gave me thoughts and words which I had never heard. It was exciting that God could use a former rejectee. Seated before me were several who had prayed for me when I had been on the verge of suicide, when I had literally walked through the valley of death. And now I was able to be a blessing to them. I could open my inmost being and pour it out openly, unashamedly, and wholeheartedly.

It's sad that people wait too long to appropriate the Word of God. I had waited almost too long. It seems that we try every possible avenue and outlet, leaving the Word for last. I was no exception. Hadn't my own mother, years before me, tried astrology, Indian guides, seances, fortune-tellers, and the whole occult scene? And that was before the popularizing of Transcendental Meditation, Eastern religions, gurus, quasi-Christian cults, psychotherapy's latest methods, and other bizarre innovations. And just like my mother finally turned to Jesus for her deliverance, I had turned to Him and the Word of God. I discovered it, after all, to be the best of all.

During my periods of exercise and meditation around the lake I had found another passage precious to my heart in Jeremiah 31:21, "Set up for yourself road-marks, place for yourself guideposts; direct your mind to the highway, the way by which you went. Return, O virgin of Israel, return to these your cities." Through the renewing of my mind, God was setting up my parameters and asking me to walk therein. He was setting my feet on His highway, not on my own pig trails. I was becoming single-minded. As a friend recently said, "It's not these twenty-five things I mess with . . . but this one thing I do!"

This calls to my mind the Scripture I learned a few weeks after I was saved—Philippians 3:13-15:

> Brethren, I do not count myself to have apprehended, but this one thing I do, forgetting those things which are behind and reaching forth unto those things which are before, I press toward the mark for the prize of the high calling of God which is in Christ Jesus.

This was at last beginning to be reality in my life after all these years.

And because I have come through this process recognizing and tearing down the strongholds of rejection in my mind, I am appropriating the reality of my acceptance and identity in Jesus Christ moment by moment, hour by hour, and day by day. I am no longer living on a performance-based acceptance that requires me to strive, strain, and struggle with all my might to please. I am in constant attendance in the classroom of renewing my mind. I am still in the process of learning how very much my mind needs to be changed, renewed, controlled, and occupied with the Word of God.

Now, I have written all this to bring you this simple procedure I have entitled "Spiritual Exercise for Renewing the Mind." See page 180. Please observe the

SPIRITUAL EXERCISE
for
RENEWING THE MIND

1. SUBMIT YOUR MIND . . . . James 4:7*a*

2. SET YOUR MIND . . . . Romans 8:6;
Colossians 3:2; Isaiah 26:3

3. RESIST THE DEVIL . . . . James 4:7*b*
Revelation 12:11

4. GIRD AND GUARD YOUR MIND . . . . 1 Peter 1:13;
Philippians 4:7

5. RELEASE YOUR MIND . . . . Philippians 2:5;
1 Corinthians 2:16; Proverbs 16:3

6. REJOICE & PRAISE . . . . Psalms 91:2; 142:7;
119:164

7. WAIT IN FAITH . . . . Isaiah 40:31

*Joy and Peace will come & you will begin to
know and express Christ's love & acceptance*
—MARK 12:30-31

illustration by that title. I go through these steps many times in a single day.

Step One: Submit Your Mind . . . James 4:7a—"Submit yourselves therefore to God . . ."

As we submit ourselves to God we are giving over our total system of thought processes.

Step Two: Set Your Mind . . . Romans 8:6—"For the mind set on the flesh is death, but the mind set on the Spirit is life and peace" (NASB)

Other helpful scriptures are:

Colossians 3:2—"Set your mind on things above and not on things that are on the earth" (NASB)

Isaiah 26:3—"Thou wilt keep him in perfect peace, whose mind is stayed on thee: because he trusteth in thee."

After we have *submitted* our minds we can then *set* our minds to trust. The result is peace.

Step Three: Resist the Devil . . . James 4:7b—"Resist the devil, and he will flee from you."

The devil is alive on planet earth—but not well! He has been overcome. Listen to the record of history, "And they overcame him [Satan] by the blood of the Lamb and the word of their testimony, and they loved not their lives even unto death." Yes, you and I have the right (and the responsibility) to resist the devil, knowing that he has no other recourse than to flee. But never make the mistake that he is fleeing from you. After we submit to God, Satan runs from God, not us!

Step Four: Gird and Guard Your Mind . . . 1 Peter 1:13—"Therefore gird your minds for action, keep sober in spirit, fix your hope on the grace to be brought to you at the revelation of Jesus Christ" (NASB). Philippians 4:7—"And the peace of God which surpasses all comprehension shall guard your hearts and minds in Christ Jesus" (NASB).

When Orientals were exhorted to gird up their loins they were being commanded to pull their garments up around their loins for maximum mobility. We need to do the same with our minds. Only when we focus on Him as our sole source are our minds kept safe and guarded.

Step Five: Release Your Mind . . . Philippians 2:5— "Let this mind be in you which was also in Christ Jesus." "Have this attitude in yourselves which was also in Christ Jesus" (NASB). 1 Corinthians 2:16—"For who hath known the mind of the Lord that he may instruct him, but we have the mind of Christ." Proverbs 16:3—"Roll your works upon the Lord. Commit and trust them wholly to Him. He will cause your thoughts to become agreeable to His will and so shall your plans be established and succeed."[1]

You and I literally have the mind of Christ. We are exhorted to *let* His mind be ours, releasing ours and accepting His. This enables God to establish our thoughts and instigate His plans.

Step Six: Rejoice and Praise . . . Psalm 91:2—"I will say of the Lord, He is my refuge and my fortress: my God; in him will I trust." Psalm 142:7—"Bring my soul out of prison that I may praise thy name. The righteous will compass me about; for thou shalt deal bountifully with me." Psalm 119:164—"Seven times a day do I praise thee because of thy righteous judgments."

Praise is the method by which I dealt and still deal with tendencies toward depression.

Step Seven: Wait in Faith . . . Isaiah 40:31—"But they that wait upon the Lord shall renew their strength. They shall mount up with wings like eagles, they shall run and not be weary; they shall walk and not faint."

Life with God is waiting, not passively but actively, in order to experience joy and peace. I assure you that, as you learn to wait on the Lord, He will begin to make these steps of renewing the mind a natural and normal exercise of reality in your life. I also guarantee you that the reality of knowing God's love and the ability to let Him express Himself to you and through you will be your life's message, too.

Come join me in teaching others how to train for liberation through the renewing of their minds.

NOTE

1. A combination of several translation ideas

14

Accepted in the Beloved

The title of this chapter was originally the working title of this book. I tell you that so you may have an idea of how important this term really is—"accepted in the beloved." I want these four words to imbed themselves in your heart. I want them in large letters on the marquee of your mind. I want them on the tape recorder of your inner ear.

You may want to reword the statement in a personal way as, "I AM ACCEPTED IN JESUS!" Just as your inner psyche has been bombarded (sometimes without your realizing it) with half-truths and outright lies for years, now there must be the constant and clear reminders that will ultimately replace all the wrong beliefs. Call it autosuggestion or self-talk, whatever you will, but do it, and keep on doing it. Someone is going to talk with you; you are going to listen to someone and do what they tell you. It may be the demons of hell, your peer group, your inner messed-up mind, or God and His Word. Those to whom you listen the most will become your models, whether you intend it or not. So, with that in mind, decide that ultimate truth is found in God and

His infallible Word, and listen, listen, listen. Then talk, talk, talk the Word—faith, hope, love, and all that we have discussed as the curriculum for the thought life of the overcomer.

Yes, I will be out front with you here as I have sought to be throughout. I admit I want you to "psyche" yourself with the Word of God. As you assume command of your mind in accord with the Word, His mind will begin to be implemented in you. Play games with yourself as far as drilling the truth into your mind. When "stinkin' thinkin' " occurs, set a Scriptural trap for the next occurrence, and do it in.

Adopt methods of keeping the truth before you at all times. Decorate your house with Scriptures. Fill the atmosphere of your home with music of praise and worship. Deliberately plan to speak of spiritual things with friends on all sorts of occasions. Play tapes of spiritual truths in your car as you travel. Write yourself (and one another) notes of spiritual truths you should always be remembering. Avoid exposure to influences that tend to infect one with the world's way of thinking. (Remember that much damage of the world's influences is done so we are hardly conscious of it at first.) You are thinking perhaps, *My, that sounds like work!* It is! And whether you know it or not this kind of work has been carried on around you ever since you were born. You have been the object of a plot hatched in hell to keep you from knowing Christ as your Savior. And ever since you have known Jesus the minions of hell have combined their energy with your flesh and the world system to keep you from knowing who you are in Him, what you have in Christ, and from exercising your heaven-confirmed rights on this earth. It's time, then, that you move into action to know and implement the eternal and unchangeable truths that will be the means of your not only becoming liberated but becoming a liberator.

I want to lay out the whole passage from which this title statement is taken so you may not only appreciate its setting but recognize its credibility. It is taken from Ephesians 1:3-6:

> Blessed be the God and Father of our Lord Jesus Christ, who hath blessed us with all spiritual blessings in heavenly places in Christ: according as he hath chosen us in him before the foundation of the world, that we should be holy and without blame before him in love, having predestinated us to adoption of children by Jesus Christ to himself, according to the good pleasure of his will, to the praise of the glory of his grace, wherein he hath made us accepted in the beloved.

That passage, in all its wonder, is a doxology to God that should be memorized and become a regular part of our praise curriculum. I want us to break it down into "bite-sized" morsels. As you read the Scripture, make it personal, using "I" or "we." Here we will use "we" because Paul does.

REASONS I HAVE TODAY TO BLESS GOD, THE FATHER OF OUR LORD JESUS CHRIST:

... HE HAS BLESSED US WITH EVERY SPIRI-
TUAL BLESSING.
... THESE BLESSINGS ARE LOCATED IN THE
HEAVENLY PLACES IN CHRIST.
... GOD HAS CHOSEN US IN CHRIST BEFORE
THE FOUNDATION OF THE WORLD.
... HIS CHOICE WAS THAT WE SHOULD BE
HOLY AND WITHOUT BLAME BEFORE
HIM IN LOVE.
... HE HAS PREDESTINATED US AS SONS BY
JESUS CHRIST TO HIMSELF.
... THIS ALL WAS TO THE GOOD PLEASURE
OF HIS WILL AND TO THE PRAISE OF THE
GLORY OF HIS GRACE.
... IT WAS BY THIS GRACE THAT HE HAS
MADE US ...
ACCEPTED IN THE BELOVED!

I have learned that, long before I was here to be
concerned about being worthy of being accepted, I was
chosen.

Long before I was around to wonder whether or not
I merited His blessings, He blessed me with every spiritual blessing in the heavenlies.

Without my having to qualify to be one of His children He predestined me for adoption!

And to the praise of the glory of His grace he MADE
ME ACCEPTED IN THE BELOVED. By an act of
His sovereign will, and not by any worthiness or work
on my part, He accepted me. He made me acceptable
and accepted me before I arrived on planet earth!

Now, how shall I close out my story? Shall I say, "To be continued"? It is far from complete. My mother is with Jesus now, and her story is complete, for she has awakened "in His likeness"!

My dad and I are in the process of being conformed to His image day by day, as are my other family members. We are daily learning to live out the truths that you have seen in the pages of this book. They are continuing to set us free.

I am realizing more and more the potent truth of Romans 8:28 that indeed all things are working for good in my life because I love God and am called according to His purpose.

I am living in the certainty that, according to Ephesians 1:6, I can work from His eternal acceptance of me in Christ and not toward it. My actions should be right, not because I want to be accepted, but because *I have been accepted.*

I am confessing that, according to 2 Corinthians 5:17, I am a new creature (creation) in Christ and that old things have passed away and all things have become new.

I am declaring that, according to Galatians 2:20, I have died, through Christ, to an old way of life and yet I live; but the life I now live I am able to live by the faith of Him who loved me and gave Himself for me.

I am affirming that my confidence in the Word of God has led me to trust what it said to me in my bondage and that the Spirit of God has used the knowledge of the truth to set me free from my deception and bondage.

I am no longer a *victim* but am now a *victor.*

I am not merely a *becomer* but am now an *overcomer.*

I no longer live in *defeat* but now live in *delight.*

I am no longer in *bondage* but am now being *liberated.*

I have come from the prison of bondage to the life of liberation in Christ.

I no longer have to perform to be accepted; I can now properly perform because I am accepted.

My daily prayer for you is that you will know these truths from God's Word and come to travel the beautiful journey . . .

FROM REJECTION TO ACCEPTANCE.

ACCEPTED IN THE BELOVED,

Barbara Taylor!

Bibliography and Suggested Reading List

AUGSBERGER, David *Caring Enough to Forgive,* Regal Books Ventura, CA (1981)

_____ *The Freedom of Forgiveness,* Moody Press, Chicago, IL (1970)

LAHAYE, Tim *How to Win Over Depression,* Zondervan Publishing House, Grand Rapids, MI (1974)

LLOYD-JONES, D. Martyn *Spiritual Depression: Its Cause and Cure,* Wm. B. Eerdmans Publishing Co. Grand Rapids, MI (1965)

SANFORD, John and Paula *The Transformation of the Inner Man,* Bridge Publishing Co., So. Plainfield, N.J. (1982)

SOLOMON, Charles R. *Ins and Outs of Rejection* Heritage House Publications, Denver CO (1976)

_____ *The Rejection Syndrome,* Tyndale House, Wheaton, IL (1982)

TAYLOR, Jack R. *After the Spirit Comes . . . ,* Broadman Press, Nashville, TN (1974)

_____ *God's New Creation,* Broadman Press, Nashville, TN (1987)

_____ *One Home Under God,* Broadman Press, Nashville, TN (1974)

_____ *Prayer: Life's Limitless Reach,* Broadman Press, Nashville, TN (1977)

_____ *The Hallelujah Factor,* Broadman Press Nashville, TN (1983)

_____ *The Key to Triumphant Living,* Broadman Press Nashville, TN (1971)

_____ *Victory Over the Devil,* Broadman Press Nashville, TN (1973)

_____ *What Every Husband Should Know,* Broadman Press Nashville TN (1981)

Tracts and Leaflets for Suggested Reading

The Mind Under the Blood, World-Wide Keswick, P.O. Box 1770, Largo, FL 33540

The Healing of the Mind, Faith and Life Publications, 623 Prosperity Lane, Andover, KS 67002

Warfare Prayer, Gospel Tract Society, Inc. P.O. Box 1118, Independence, MO 64051

Preparation for Spiritual Reproduction, Gerry Leonard, Christ's Life Concept, 2700 Helmer Court, Orlando, FL 32806